MOTION

Order of precedence	Interrupt Speaker?	Requires a Second?	Debatable?	Vote needed?	Can renew at same meeting?	What motion can be applied to it?
PRIVILEGED MOTIONS						
1. Fix time to adjourn	N	Y	L	M	Y	11,15
2. Adjourn	N	Y	N	M	Y	none
3. Recess	N	Y	L	M	Y	11
4. Question of privilege	Y	N	N	N	Y	all
5. Call for Orders of Day	Y	N	N	N	Y	none
SUBSIDIARY MOTIONS						
6. Lay on the Table	N	Y	N	M	Y	none
7. Previous Question (vote immediately)	N	Y	N	Y 2/3	Y	15
8. Limit Debate	N	Y	L	Y 2/3	Y	11,15
9. Postpone Definitely	N	Y	L	M	Y	7,8,11,15
10. Refer to Committee	N	Y	L	M	Y	7,8,11,15
11. Amend	N	Y	Y	M	N	7,8,11,15
12. Postpone Indefinitely	N	Y	Y	M	N	7,8,15
MAIN MOTIONS						
13. A General Main Motion	N	Y	Y	M	N	all
Specific Main Motions						
14. Take from the Table	N	Y	N	M	Y	none
15. Reconsider	Y	Y	Y	M	N	6,7,8,12
16. Reconsider and Have Entered on Minutes	Y	Y	N	X	N	none
17. Rescind	N	Y	Y	Y 2/3	N	all
18. Expunge	N	Y	Y	Y 2/3	N	all
19. Adopt a Resolution	N	Y	Y	M	N	all
20. Create Orders of Day	N	Y	Y	M	Y	all
INCIDENTAL MOTIONS (no order of precedence)						
21. Suspend Rules	N	Y	N	Y 2/3	N	none
22. Withdraw a Motion	N	N	N	N	Y	none
23. Point of Order	Y	N	N	N	N	none
24. Request for Information	Y	N	N	N	N	none
25. Appeal from Decision of the Chair	Y	Y	L	M	N	all except 11
26. Division of the House	Y	N	N	N	N	none
27. Division of a Question	N	N	N	N	N	none

KEY
Y yes
N no
L limited
M majority
X not until called up

For further reference, see Chapters 4 and 10

Modern Rules of Order

Originally published as
CUSHING'S MANUAL OF PARLIAMENTARY PRACTICE

BY LUTHER S. CUSHING

A CREST REPRINT

FAWCETT PUBLICATIONS, INC., GREENWICH, CONN.
MEMBER OF AMERICAN BOOK PUBLISHERS COUNCIL, INC.

Contents

CHAPTER VIII

CHAPTER IX

CHAPTER X

Preface

This book is intended as a **Manual for Deliberative Assemblies** of every description, whether legislative in character or otherwise.

Members of legislative bodies, who may use this book, should keep in mind the fact that what is known as the **Common Parliamentary Law**, for reasons of convenience and expediency, has undergone more or less modification, and is subject to special rules, in the proceedings of various legislative bodies.

In order to obtain a general idea of the proceedings of an ordinary society or organization, the attention of the reader is called to the "**Exemplar, Demonstrating the Proceedings of a Typical Society, etc.,**" on page 153.

For quick reference on motions, the special chart on page one will prove useful.

A close study of the Index, page 183, is recommended to the reader, as a means of familiarizing himself with the contents of the book.

Modern Rules
of Order

Parliamentary Law

The fundamentals of **Parliamentary Law,** as practiced in the Congress of the United States and other legislative and deliberative bodies, originated in the British Parliament as a method of procedure for the orderly regulation of customs and rules for conducting the deliberations and business in that historic institution.

In the United States, however, many innovations and changes have been made in the written rules by some legislative bodies. These have been adopted by them as improvements and expedients, applicable to complex situations, existing in such bodies, with which others were not confronted. Although two houses of the same legislature may not at all times agree in their practice, the departure from pre-existing principles is not radical, but preferably for practicability, in cases where the rules or customs are sufficiently flexible to admit of modifications.

The order of precedence of motions, for instance, differs in both houses of Congress. In the House of Representatives the previous question is admitted, but not so in the Senate. Because of these variations, and to become familiar with the particular manner of conducting business in any given legislative body, it is necessary to consult the Legislative Manual of each body.

The almost countless non-legislative societies and organizations existing in the United States—and which are deliberative in character—have customs and rules governing their methods of procedure framed from the common parliamentary law and the usages current in the United States, and subject to which their deliberations and proceedings are conducted.

Deviating from the old parliamentary law, the House of Representatives, under stress of an enormous growth of business, was driven to the necessity of changing its rules and practice, thereby permitting a majority to suppress the debate, if there has been previous debate, and to limit it to forty minutes if there has been no previous debate; and furthermore, to suppress a question for the session without any debate.

This departure from the old parliamentary law is neither necessary nor advisable in ordinary deliberative bodies, where the right should be maintained to have questions thoroughly discussed before the members are required to act upon them. There could be an exception in the event that a majority of at least two-thirds of the assembly is ready to take immediate action; and in that case the motion to lay on the table should operate only in consonance with the parliamentary provision and intent for temporarily laying a question aside.

The practice of Congress is very generally followed by deliberative bodies in this country in many respects, notwithstanding its deviations in some instances from old parliamentary law. Therefore, in such bodies, devoid of governing rules, the motion to adjourn would be considered undebatable when it does not dissolve the assembly; and if the previous question were negatived, debate upon the subject would go on. Under old parliamentary law the subject would be dismissed at once. Likewise when there is a motion before the assembly to commit or postpone definitely or indefinitely, the previous question may be moved; whereas in conformity with the old parliamentary law the previous question may not be moved.

The same rank, under the old parliamentary law, is assigned to motions for the previous question, to commit, to postpone definitely or indefinitely, and while any one of them is pending no other one can be moved. This same order of rank obtains in the House, whereas in the Senate the motion for the previous question is not admitted, and the ''to postpone indefinitely'' is ranked above all others. The practice of the House in this respect has been very extensively adopted in the United States, and the practice of the House in general may be taken as a criterion of the practice of parliamentary law in this country. In certain instances there can be exception, when the pressure of business in the House demands modification of the practice, and complex problems arise to which other deliberative bodies are not subject.

Purposes for Which Deliberative Assemblies Are Constituted

The purposes, whatever they may be, for which a deliberative assembly of any kind is constituted, can only be effected by ascertaining the sense or will of the assembly, in reference to the several subjects submitted to it, and by embodying that sense or will in an intelligible, authentic, and authoritative form. To do this, it is necessary, in the first place, that the assembly should be promptly constituted and organized. Secondly, it should conduct its proceedings according to certain rules, and agreeably to certain forms, which experience has shown to be the best adapted to the purpose.

Some deliberative assemblies, especially those which consist of permanently established bodies, such as municipal and other corporations, are usually constituted and organized at least in part, in virtue of certain legal provisions. Others, of an occasional or temporary character, such as conventions and political meetings, constitute and organize themselves on their assembling together for the purposes of their appointment.

Most Convenient Mode of Organizing an Assembly

The most usual and convenient mode of organizing a deliberative assembly is the following:—The members being assembled together, in the place, and at the time appointed for their meeting, one of them, addressing himself to the others, requests them to come to order. The members seat themselves. The member who has spoken now suggests the propriety and necessity of their being organized, before proceeding to business, and requests the members to nominate some person to act as chairman of the meeting. After a name or names has been mentioned, he declares that such a person (whose name was first heard by him) is nominated for chairman. He then puts a question that the person so named be requested to take the chair. If this question should be decided in the negative, another nomination is then to be called for, and a question put upon the name mentioned (being that of some other person) as before, and so on until a choice is effected. When a chairman is elected, he takes the chair, and proceeds in the same manner to complete the organization of the assembly, by the choice of a secretary and such other officers, if any, as may be deemed necessary.

Permanent Organization

An organization, thus effected, may be, and frequently is, sufficient for all the purposes of the meeting. If, for any reason, it is desired to have a greater number of officers, or to have them selected with more deliberation, it is the practice to organize temporarily, in the manner above mentioned, and then to refer the subject of a permanent organization, and the selection of persons to be nominated for the several offices, to a committee. It is upon the committee's report that the meeting proceeds to organize itself, conformably thereto, or in such other manner as it thinks proper.

Officers

The presiding officer is usually denominated the *president*, and the recording officer the *secretary;* though sometimes these officers are designated, respectively, as the *chairman* and *clerk*. It is not unusual, besides a president, to have one or more vice-presidents, who take the chair, occasionally, in the absence of the president, or when he withdraws from the chair to take part in the proceedings as a member. At other times, though occupying seats with the president, they act merely as members. It is frequently the case, also, that several persons are appointed secretaries, in which case, the first named is considered as the principal officer. All the officers are, ordinarily, members of the assembly*; and, as such, entitled to participate in the proceedings; except that the presiding officer does not usually engage in the debate, and votes only when the assembly is equally divided.

Members Duly Elected

In all deliberative assemblies, the members of which are chosen or appointed to represent others, it is necessary, before proceeding to business, to ascertain who are duly elected and returned as members. This is in order that no person may be admitted to participate in the proceedings who is not regularly authorized to do so, and also that a list of the members may be made for the use of the assembly and its officers.

Report on Credentials of Members

The proper time for this investigation is after the temporary and before the permanent organization; or, when the assembly is permanently organized, in the first instance, before it proceeds to the transaction of any other business. The most convenient mode of conducting it is by the appointment of a committee to receive and report upon the credentials of the members.† The same committee may also be charged with the investigation of rival claims, where any such are presented.

Question as to Right of Membership

When a question arises, involving the right of a member to his seat, such member is entitled to be

* In legislative bodies, the clerk is seldom or never a member; and, in some, the presiding officer is not a member; as, for example, in the Senate of the United States, the Senate of New York, and in some other State senates.

† In reporting the list of members with proper credentials, the committee may report the names of contestants with recommendations for the action of the assembly, and these may be followed, modified, or rejected.

heard on the question, and he is then to withdraw from the assembly until it is decided. However, if, by the indulgence of the assembly, he remains in his place during the discussion, he ought neither to take any further part in it, nor to vote when the question is proposed. It is a fundamental rule of all deliberative assemblies, that those members whose rights as such are not yet set aside, constitute a judicial tribunal to decide upon the cases of those whose rights of membership are called in question. Care should always be taken, therefore, in the selection of the officers, and in the appointment of committees, to name only those persons whose rights as members are not objected to.

Right of an Assembly to Its Place of Meeting

The place where an assembly is held being in its possession, and rightfully appropriated to its use, no person is entitled to be present therein, but by the consent of the assembly. Consequently, if any person refuse to withdraw, when ordered to do so, or conduct himself in a disorderly or improper manner, the assembly may unquestionably employ sufficient force to remove such person from the meeting.

Assemblies Subject to Rules

Every deliberative assembly, by the mere fact of its being assembled and constituted, does thereby necessarily adopt and become subject to those rules and forms of proceeding, without which it would be impossible for it to accomplish the purposes of its creation. It is perfectly competent, however, and not unusual, for every such body—and where the business is of considerable interest and importance, or likely to require some time for its accomplishment—to adopt also certain special rules for the regulation of its proceedings. Where this is the case, these latter supersede the ordinary parliamentary rules, in reference to all points to which they relate; or add to them in those particulars in reference to which there is no parliamentary rule; leaving what may be called the common parliamentary law in full force in all other respects.

Rules of Parliamentary Proceedings

The rules of parliamentary proceedings in this country are derived from, and are essentially the same with those of the British parliament; though, in order to adapt these rules to the circumstances and wants of our legislative assemblies, they have, in some few respects, been changed; in others, differently applied, and in others, again, extended beyond their original intention. To these rules, each legislative assembly is accustomed to add a code of its own, by which, in conjunction with the former, its proceedings are regulated. The rules thus adopted by the several legislative assemblies, having been renewed in successive legislatures—with such extensions, modifications and additions as have been from time to time thought necessary—the result is that a system of parliamentary rules has been established in each state, different in some particulars from those of every other state, but yet founded on and embracing all the essential rules of the common parliamentary law.

Parliamentary Practice Applied

The rules of procedure in each state are best known by the citizens of that state. And so it has sometimes happened in deliberative assemblies that the proceedings have been conducted not merely according to the general parliamentary law, but also in conformity with the peculiar system of the state in which the assembly was sitting, or of whose citizens it was composed. This, however, is erroneous; as no occasional assembly can ever be subject to any other rules than those which are of general application, or which it specially adopts for its own government. The rules adopted and practiced upon by a legislative assembly do not thereby acquire the character of general laws.

The judgment, opinion, sense, or will of a deliberate assembly is expressed, according to the nature of the subject, either by a resolution, order, or vote. When it commands, it is by an *order*. Facts, principles, its own opinions or purposes, are most properly expressed in the form of a *resolution*. The term *vote* may be applied to the result of every question decided by the assembly. In whatever form, however, a question is proposed, or by whatever name it may be called, the mode of proceeding is the same.

Ascertaining the Will of the Assembly

The judgment or will of any number of persons, considered as an aggregate body, is that which is evidenced by the consent or agreement of the greater number of them. The only mode by which this can be ascertained, in reference to any particular subject, is for some one of them to begin by submitting to the others a proposition, expressed in such a form of words, that, if assented to by the requisite number, it will purport to express the judgment or will of the assembly. This proposition will then form a basis for further proceedings of the assembly; to be assented to, rejected or modified, according as it expresses or not, or may be made to express the sense of a majority of the members. The different proceedings which take place, from the first submission of a proposition, through all the changes it may undergo until the final decision of the assembly upon it, constitute the subject of the rules of debate and proceeding in deliberate assemblies.

Functions of Members of an Assembly Not Limited

If the proceedings of a deliberative assembly were confined to the making of propositions by the individual members, and their acceptance or rejection by the votes of the assembly, there would be very little occasion for rules in such a body. But this is not the case. The functions of the members are not limited to giving an affirmative or negative to such questions as are proposed to them. When a proposition is made, if it be not agreed to or rejected at once, the assembly may be unwilling to consider and act upon it at all. On the other hand, it may wish to postpone the consideration of the subject to a future time; or it may be willing to adopt the proposition with certain modifications; or, lastly, approving the subject-matter, but finding it presented in so crude, imperfect or objectionable a form, that it cannot in that state be considered at all, the assembly may desire to have the proposition further examined and digested, before being presented. In order to enable the assembly to take whichever of the courses above indicated it may think proper, and then to dispose of every proposition in a suitable manner, certain motions or forms of question have been invented, which are perfectly adapted for the purpose, and are in common use in all deliberative assemblies.

Object of Meeting

For the government of a permanent association the rules of procedure are sometimes established by law and sometimes by the association. When the organization of a temporary association is perfected the object of the meeting is asked by the chairman. Then some one may state the object and move that a committee be appointed to prepare the resolutions and report them. Sometimes at a public meeting there may have been already prepared and offered by some one a series of resolutions. The rules of procedure are not always the same, but may vary according to the object of the association.

Manner of Procedure

Whenever a person rises to address the chair, the chairman answers, asking the name of the speaker, unless he knows it, in which case he addresses the speaker by name. Having gotten the floor and been recognized, the speaker may offer his resolutions, should he have any, explaining them and moving their adoption. At the same time he will hand them to the secretary or chairman, when the assembly is not a permanent body. When it is a permanent organization, such as legislative and other like bodies, all resolutions and papers pertaining to the business of the assembly are sent to the secretary's desk.

Resolutions

To make the meaning of resolutions perfectly clear and intelligible to every one present, the chairman may of his own accord, or by request of some one, require the secretary to read them aloud. When this has been done the chairman announces that the question is upon the adoption of the resolutions which have been read. The chairman then asks, as a matter of form in order to bring the resolutions to the attention of the body: "Are you ready for the question?" But not until discussion has followed; or some one has something to say or offer an amendment; or the assemblage remains silent is the vote taken. In that case the chairman puts the question as follows: "All those who are in favor of the adoption of the resolutions just read will say 'aye.' " When those in favor of adopting the resolutions have so signified their will by answering "aye," the chairman says: "All those opposed to the adoption of the resolutions just read will say 'no.' " The chairman then announces the result of the vote. If the ayes are in the majority he says: "The resolutions are adopted."

Committee on Resolutions

The chairman asks of how many the committee shall consist. He then states the one or more numbers that may have been mentioned and secures a vote, beginning with the largest or the smallest number, and taking the number decided upon. This is followed by a question as to how they are to be appointed, and if it is decided by those present that the chairman makes the appointments, he proceeds to act accordingly and makes the selections. The chairman of the committee is usually appointed first, he having made the motion.

Naming the Committee

Sometimes the committee is made up "by nomination" unless the matter is voted upon, which rarely occurs. Unless by unanimous agreement no person can name more than one in naming members of a committee, and each nomination is voted upon, and there is one vote on all appointees when the chairman appoints.

Committee Reports

By the chairman, or the member first appointed, arrangements are made for all the members to meet to consider what to report, and while this is being done the meeting may adjourn "subject to the call of the chairman," or remain in session, as it may prefer. The business of making the report being completed, the chairman of the committee that drafted the resolutions notifies the chairman that the committee is ready to report. The chairman then announces: "The meeting will now listen to the report of the committee." He then proceeds to read it, after which he gives it to the secretary or presiding officer, which automatically dissolves the committee without further action.

Action on the Report

There is now a move made by some one to adopt or accept the report. In some bodies two processes are in practice: one to accept and one to adopt. A report can be received and the committee discharged without adopting the report, and thereby it becomes the sense of all.

At this stage of the proceedings the report may come up for debate, acceptance, rejection or modification. Final action being taken, some one makes a motion to adjourn and the chairman announces the result.

Organization of Continuous Bodies

One form of such bodies is where the membership is composed of some exisiting or continuing members and new members. As stated by Chief Justice Lowrie in Kerr v. Trego, 57 Pa. 297: "In all cases where part of the public body remains, and is to be completed by the reception of new members, it remains as an organized nucleus, and in its organized form it receives the new members and then proceeds to the election of new officers, if any are to be elected. The old nucleus is not dissolved by the new incoming elements, but these are added to it, and the whole body proceeds to the exercise of all its functions.''

On the convening of a new Congress, where the vice-president does not appear and the last president pro tem does, the United States Senate is organized in this manner and the practice is followed generally throughout this country.

CHAPTER I

Of Certain Preliminary Matters

Before entering upon the subject of the forms and
rules of proceeding in the transaction of business, it
will be convenient to consider certain matters of a
preliminary nature, which are more or less essential
to the regularity, despatch and efficiency of the proceedings.

Quorum

A quorum of an assembly consists of the number
present, and not the number voting. In order that
business may be transacted legally, a quorum must
always be present.

In a mass meeting a quorum consists of the number
present at the time; that being the number constituting the membership on that occasion.

Unless in case the by-laws stipulate a smaller quorum, the quorum in a body of delegates consists of a
majority of the enrolled delegates attending the convention.

In any other deliberative assembly, unless the by-
laws provide for a smaller quorum, a majority of all
the members constitutes the quorum.

In organizations or societies, whose by-laws, if any,
do not provide for the creation of a quorum, the quorum is composed of all those who attend the meeting;
but in case only that such meeting is either one that
has been properly called, or is a stated meeting.

It is advisable, that in all ordinary organizations
and societies, the by-laws should provide for a quorum of a sufficient number to assure a full comple-
ment of attendance at the meetings under all
ordinary circumstances. In such assemblies the chairman should not take the chair until a quorum is present, or in default of obtaining one. When failure to

obtain a quorum occurs, there can be no business transacted except the devising of necessary measures to obtain one, and take up such matters as the time to which to adjourn, and to take a recess or to adjourn.

When a quorum is not present unanimous consent cannot be given, which renders null and void any notice given at that time.

In the absence of a quorum at the time specified, where an assembly is empowered to compel the attendance of members, the assembly may order a call of the house and compel those found absent to attend, or, at its option, the assembly may adjourn.

A committee of the whole, in the absence of a quorum, would be affected in the same manner as the assembly. Its only recourse would be to rise and report to the assembly, which would then take an adjournment. In any other committee, unless otherwise ordered by the assembly, the majority constitutes the quorum and such committee cannot transact business until a quorum is present.

The same rule governing committees with respect to a quorum is likewise applicable to directors, boards of trustees, managers, etc. Unless it is so specifically stipulated in the by-laws, these cannot determine for themselves whether or not they are empowered to act as a committee or board without a quorum, as their powers are delegated to them as a body; and their quorum, or the number that shall be present, in order that they may act, has already been determined for them by the established source of authority.

As stated above, no question can be decided without a quorum, except those already mentioned. Yet a member speaking for the purpose of making a point of no quorum cannot be interrupted, and unless some one raises the point while no one is speaking, the debate may go in the absence of a quorum.

Unless the attendance at a meeting is reasonably representative of the entire numerical strength of the membership or body, it is not considered the best policy to transact business of an important nature, even though a competent quorum be present; the exception is when previous notice of intention to act upon such business has been announced.

The act of amending a rule providing for a quorum should be exercised with considerable allowance for consequences in the proceedings of many organizations and societies, in which it would be very difficult to secure a quorum to adopt a new rule, should the existing rule be struck out first; for in that case the quorum becomes instantly a majority of all the members. To avoid such an embarrassing contingency, the amendment should be made by striking out the whole rule, or certain words; or by introducing a new rule, or inserting certain other words. Then the vote may be taken on the amendment as on one question.

Rules and Orders

Providing Rules for Assembly

Every deliberative assembly, as has already been observed, is, by the fact alone of its existence, subject to those rules of proceeding, without which it could not accomplish the purpose of its creation. It may also provide rules for itself, either in the form of a general code established beforehand, or by the adoption, from time to time, during its sitting, of such special rules as it may find necessary.

Mode of Amending

When a code of rules is adopted beforehand, it is usual also to provide therein as to the mode in which they may be amended, repealed, or dispensed with. Where there is no such provision, it will be competent for the assembly to act at any time, and in the usual manner, upon questions of amendment or repeal; but in reference to dispensing with a rule, or suspending it, in a particular case, if there is no express provision on the subject, it seems that it can only be done by general consent.

Enforcement of Rules

When any rule, adopted by the assembly, or which is in force, relative to its manner of proceeding, is disregarded or infringed, every member has the right to take notice thereof and to require that the presiding officer, or any other whose duty it is, shall carry such rule into execution. In that case, the rule must be enforced, at once, without debate or delay. It is then too late to alter, repeal, or suspend the rule; so long as any one member insists upon its execution, it must be enforced.

Time of Meeting

Every assembly, which is not likely to finish its business at one sitting, will find it convenient to come to some order or resolution beforehand, as to the time of reassembling, after an adjournment; it being generally embarrassing to fix upon the hour for this purpose, at the time when the sitting is about to close, and in connection with the motion to adjourn.

Session

A session of an assembly is, in fact, the same as one meeting, although it may be prolonged for an indefinite number of days, weeks or months, and terminates by adjournment, *"sine die," i. e., "without day."*

The continuity of the meetings from day to day is not broken by intermediate adjournments and recesses taken; whereas, in the case of a permanent organization, whose by-laws provide for regular meetings at stated times, each meeting is a separate session; but which, however, may be continued as the same session by adjournment to another day.

Succinctly stated: A temporary adjournment or recess terminates a "meeting" of an assembly; but a "session" of an assembly may extend throughout a number of meetings, and terminates only with an adjournment "without day."

Usually a motion to adjourn serves to close a meeting, and the time of the next meeting is provided for either by the rules of the society or by a resolution. However, if there should be no meeting till the time for the next regular meeting, as provided in the by-laws, the adjournment, in that case, closes the session, and is tantamount to an adjournment *"without day."* On the other hand, if the time for the next meeting had been previously fixed by a direct vote, or by adopting a program of exercise covering several meetings or days, the adjournment would be in force to a certain time in either case, and would close the meeting while not closing the session.

At any session of a society a rule or resolution of a permanent nature may be adopted by a majority vote, and until rescinded will continue effective. But a standing rule of this kind may be suspended by a majority vote of a future session, in so far as it effects that session by interference with its rights. Furthermore, it can be rescinded by a majority vote, providing that notice to that effect had been previously given; or it can be rescinded without notice by a majority of the whole membership, or by a two-thirds vote.

Principle of Decision

Majority Rule

The principle, upon which the decisions of all aggregate bodies, such as councils, corporations, and deliberative assemblies, are made, is that of the majority of votes or suffrages. This rule holds not only in reference to questions and subjects, which admit only of an affirmative on one side, and a negative on the other, but also in reference to elections in which more than two persons may receive the suffrages.

A proposition is always carried by a majority vote when a quorum is present, unless there should pre-exist some special rule to the contrary. A judicial decision (62 New Hamp. Rep. 383) touching upon this subject has been handed down as follows: "The exercise of law-making power is not stopped by the mere silence and inaction of some of the law-makers who are present. An arbitrary, technical and exclusive method of ascertaining whether a quorum is present operating to prevent the performance of official duty and obstruct the business of government is no part of our common law.''

Rule of Majority Controlled

But this rule may be controlled by a special rule in reference to some particular subject or question, by which any less number than a majority may be admitted, or any greater number required to express the will of the assembly. Thus, it is frequently provided, in legislative assemblies, that one-third or one-fourth only of the members shall be sufficient to require the taking of a question by yeas and nays,* and, on the other hand, that no alteration shall take place in any of the rules and orders, without the consent of at least two-thirds, or even a larger number.

But, as authoritatively set forth in ''Dillon on Municipal Corporations,'' as referred to such bodies, a minority cannot bind a majority. To quote from Dillon: ''As a general rule, it may be stated, that not only where the corporate power resides in a select body, as a city council, but where it has been delegated to a committee or agents, then, in the absence of special provisions otherwise, a minority of the select body, or of the committee or agents, are powerless to bind the majority to do any valid act. If all the members of the select body or committee or if all of the agents are assembled, or if all have been duly notified, and the minority refuse or neglect to meet with the others, a majority of those present may act, provided those present constitute a majority of the whole number.

* The quota of members, in the United States, having the power to demand that a question be put by yeas and nays, is decided both for Congress and for State Legislatures by *constitutional provision.*

In the case of the Constitution of the United States the number is one-fifth; and while some State Constitutions give this power to one-fifth, others give it to three members, some to two, and some to one member.

In other words, in such a case, a major part of the whole is necessary to constitute a quorum, and a majority of the quorum may act. If the major part withdraw so as to leave no quorum, the power of the minority to act is, in general, considered to cease."

CHAPTER II

Of the Officers

The Necessary Officers

The usual and necessary officers of a deliberative assembly are those already mentioned, namely, a presiding, and a recording, officer. Both of these are elected or appointed by the assembly itself, and removable at its pleasure. These officers are always to be elected by absolute majorities, even in those states in which elections are usually effected by a plurality. This is because, being removable at the pleasure of the assembly, if any number short of a majority were to elect, a person elected by such less number would not be able to retain his office for a moment; inasmuch as he might be instantly removed therefrom, on a question made for that purpose, by the votes of those who had voted for other persons on the election. And it is essential to the due and satisfactory performance of the functions of these officers that they should possess the confidence of the assembly, which they cannot be said to do, unless they have the suffrages of at least a majority.

The Presiding Officer—His Duties

The principal duties of this officer are the following:

To open the sitting, at the time to which the assembly is adjourned, by taking the chair and calling the members to order.

To announce the business before the assembly in the order in which it is to be acted upon.

To receive and submit, in the proper manner, all motions and propositions presented by the members.

To put to vote all questions, which are regularly moved, or necessarily arise in the course of the proceedings, and to announce the result.

To restrain the members, when engaged in debate, within the rules of order.

To enforce on all occasions the observance of order and decorum among the members.

To receive all messages and other communications and announce them to the assembly.

To authenticate, by his signature, when necessary, all the acts, orders, and proceedings of the assembly.

To inform the assembly when necessary, or when referred to for the purpose, on a point of order or practice.

To name the members (when directed to do so in a particular case, or when it is made a part of his general duty by a rule) who are to serve on committees; and, in general.

To represent and stand for the assembly, declaring its will, and in all things obeying implicitly its commands.

Duty of Vice-President in Absence of the President

If the assembly is organized by the choice of a president and vice-presidents, it is the duty of one of the latter to take the chair, in case of the absence of the president from the assembly, or of his withdrawing from the chair for the purpose of participating in the proceedings.

President or Chairman Pro Tempore

Where but one presiding officer is appointed, in the first instance, his place can only be supplied, in case of his absence, by the appointment of a president or chairman *pro tempore*. In the choice of this officer, who ought to be elected before any other business is done, it is the duty of the secretary to conduct the proceedings.

When Presiding Officer Should Sit or Stand

The presiding officer may read sitting, but should rise to state a motion, or put a question to the assembly.

The Recording Officer—His Duties

The principal duties of this officer consist in taking notes of all the proceedings, and in making true entries in his journal of all "the things done and past" in the assembly; but he is not, in general, required to take minutes of "particular men's speeches," or to make entries of things merely proposed or moved, without coming to a vote. He is to enter what is done and past, but not what is said or moved. This is the rule in legislative assemblies. In others, though the spirit of the rule ought to be observed, it is generally expected of the secretary, that his record shall be both a journal and in some sort a report of the proceedings.*

The Secretary—His Duties

It is also the duty of the secretary to read all papers, etc., which may be ordered to be read; to call the roll of the assembly, and take note of those who are absent, when a call is ordered; to call the roll and note the answers of the members, when a question is taken by yeas and nays; to notify committees of their appointment and of the business referred to them; and to authenticate by his signature (sometimes alone and sometimes in conjunction with the president) all the acts, orders, and proceedings of the assembly. The clerk may, on motion, enter the protest of any member, and his reason therefor, against a measure, on the journal. In some states this right is secured to members by constitutional provision. In 1834 President Jackson sent a protest to the Senate against some condemnatory resolutions passed against him by that body, but it refused to receive his protest, declaring that it was a breach of privilege.

* In the United States House of Representatives the roll of membership is made up by the clerk, who also presides until a speaker is elected, which election he announces to the assembly.

Custody of All Documents, etc.

The clerk is also charged with the custody of all the papers and documents of every description belonging to the assembly, as well as the journal of its proceedings, and is to let none of them be taken from the table by any member or other person, without the leave or order of the assembly.

Pro Tempore Appointment of Secretary

When but a single secretary or clerk is appointed, his place can only be supplied, during his absence, by the appointment of some one to act *pro tempore.* When several persons are appointed, this inconvenience is not likely to occur.

Posture of Clerk

The clerk should stand while reading or calling the assembly.

The Minutes

The proceedings of a deliberative assembly are recorded in a book kept for that purpose and which is known as "The Minutes," or "The Record," or "The Journal."

The data which are usually entered in the minutes are: (1) Name of the assembly; (2) date of meeting; (3) place of meeting (if it is not in a permanently established place); (4) kind of meeting, *i.e.,* whether *regular, stated, special, adjourned regular,* or *adjourned special;* (5) whether or not the regular chairman and secretary are present, and if not, the names of their substitutes; (6) whether or not the minutes of the previous meeting were approved, or were not read at all; (7) all main motions that were not withdrawn; (8) all appeals and points of order that were not withdrawn or lost; (9) and when the meeting is for business only, it is customary to record the hours of meeting and adjournment; and also the name of the member who may have introduced a main motion, but not that of the member who seconded it.

When the minutes of a society or organized body are published, they should be signed by both the president and secretary.

When it is not a usual practice to approve the minutes at a following meeting, there should be written in the minutes at the close of each meeting the word "approved" and also the date of the approval, and these notations should be signed by the secretary.*

The character of a meeting, and whether or not the minutes are to be published, are essential considerations in the manner of keeping them. In many societies, board meetings, etc., there is no occasion to report debates, as the only things pertinent are those acts which are accomplished by the assembly, and not what has been said by the members. In such cases the duty of the secretary is confined mainly to making a record of what has *actually been done*. When the secretary has recorded the essential features of the proceedings, and when a count has been ordered, or the vote is by ballot, the number of votes on each side should be entered. If the vote is by yeas and nays, the names of those voting on each side should be entered.

The report of the committee of the whole should be entered in the minutes; but the proceedings of the committee, or while acting as if in committee of the whole, should not be entered in the minutes.

The proceedings should be kept in the usual way when a question is considered informally—the debate being the only informality. When a report containing resolutions has been agreed to, the resolutions should be recorded complete as finally adopted by the assembly, substantially in the manner following: "A report

* It is advisable, in many organizations, for the secretary to provide himself with a pocket memorandum book and to enter therein his original notes. This book he should take with him to every meeting and when these notes are corrected and approved they should be copied into the permanent records, and after the original notes have been carefully compared with the entry of the same in the permanent records, the minutes, in order to guard against errors in copying, should be signed by both the president and secretary.

with a series of resolutions has been submitted by the committee on — — — —, and after discussion and amendment the resolutions were adopted [here the resolutions as adopted should be entered]." Where a report is of unusual importance and the assembly orders it "to be entered in the minutes," the secretary should make a complete copy of it upon the record.

The minutes should be read at the opening of each meeting, and corrected and approved, when regular meetings are held weekly, monthly or quarterly; but they should be read at the opening of business each day when the meetings are held for several consecutive days with recesses during the day. When long periods of time intervene between meetings—say several months or a year—and the minutes of a previous meeting were not read, they should be read and approved, before final adjournment of the next meeting, or when not feasible to do so, then they should be turned over for correction and approval to the executive committee, or to a specially authorized committee, and the chairman of one or the other of these two committees should affix his signature to the record, after the usual signatures, and the word "approved," and the date also should be entered. When minutes have not been read because deemed not necessary at the time, they may be afterwards taken up, and at any time, providing no other matter is pending, and if not disposed of previously they are taken up at the following meeting of the assembly before the reading of subsequent minutes.

Being undebatable and requiring a majority vote only, the motion to waive the reading of the minutes is to all intents and purposes equivalent to laying them on the table.

Minutes to Be Published

In addition to a complete record of what has been accomplished, minutes for publication should embody the names of the speakers on both sides of all questions, and where the addresses are not given in full, or written copies of them furnished, abstracts of the addresses should be contained in the copy for publication. When it is desirable to publish the proceedings in full, as in some large annual assemblies and conventions, a stenographer is usually employed as assistant to the secretary.

There should be no departure from the exact language of reports to be printed, which have been submitted by committees. The minutes should show such action as was taken by the assembly in relation to them. Moreover, they may be printed with any supplementary matter in italics, or any matter that is struck out, if the same be enclosed in brackets. But in such case—and in order that it may be clearly shown what the committee reported and also exactly what the assembly adopted or endorsed—there should be inserted an explanatory note preceding the report or resolutions.

A Typical Form of the Minutes

The regular business meeting of the Michigan Fruit Growers Association was called to order at 10 A. M. on March 3, 1963, in Assembly Hall, Detroit, Michigan, by the President, Samuel Doane.

Following the roll call, the minutes of the previous meeting, held on February 10, 1963, were read.

Mr. Fallcott called the assembly's attention to an error in attributing to Mr. William Jackson a motion that was proposed by Mr. Arthur Elliott. This correction having been made, the minutes were declared approved.

The following report was tendered by Mr. Ephraim Baxter, chairman of the committee for securing better refrigerating facilities for the preservation of fruit in transportation. A motion to accept this report was carried and consideration of the appended resolutions was postponed until the next meeting.

A motion was made, seconded, and carried to postpone all unfinished business until the next meeting.

It was moved by Mr. Edgar Wallace, seconded, and carried, that $125,000 be appropriated to erect a building to be known as the **Permanent Headquarters of the Michigan Fruit Growers Association.**

It was moved by Mr. Thomas Cole, and seconded,

that a special meeting be held on March 28, 1963, for the purpose of considering the increase in freight rates. It was moved, seconded, and carried, that the vote on this question be taken by *Yeas* and *Nays*. The vote was taken, with the following result:

Yeas 185—Nays 160. The motion was carried by 25 votes.

A vote of thanks was accorded to Prof. Jameson who addressed the meeting on the subject of Successful Grafting.

The meeting adjourned at 12:30 P. M.

Respectfully submitted,

ALBERT WARFIELD,

Secretary.

Approved by vote of the **Michigan Fruit Growers Association.**

CHAPTER III

Of the Rights and Duties of the Members

Equality of Members

The rights and duties of the members of a deliberative assembly, as regards one another, are founded in and derived from the principle of their absolute equality among themselves. Every member, however humble he may be, has the same right with every other, to submit his propositions to the assembly—to explain and recommend them in discussion—and to have them patiently examined and deliberately decided upon by the assembly. On the other hand, it is the duty of every one so to conduct himself, both in debate, and in his general deportment in the assembly, as not to obstruct any other member, in the enjoyment of his equal rights. The rights and duties of the members require to be explained only in reference to words spoken in debate (whether spoken of a member or otherwise) and to general deportment. The first will be most conveniently noticed in the chapter on debate; the other will be considered in this chapter.

Observance of Decorum

The observance of decorum by the members of a deliberative assembly is not only due to themselves and to one another, as gentlemen assembled together to deliberate on matters of common importance and interest, but is also essential to the regular and satisfactory proceeding of such an assembly. The rules on this subject, though generally laid down with reference to decorum in debate, are equally applicable whether the assembly be at the time engaged in debate or not; and therefore, it may be stated, generally, that no member is to disturb another, or the assembly itself, by hissing, coughing, or spitting; by speaking or whispering to other members; by standing up to the interruption of others; by passing between the presiding officer and a member speaking; going across the assembly room, or walking up and down in it; taking books or papers from the table, or writing there.

Breaches of Decorum

All these breaches of decorum are doubtless aggravated by being committed while the assembly is engaged in debate, though equally contrary to the rules of propriety under any other circumstances. Assaults, by one member upon another—threats—challenges—affrays, etc., are also high breaches of decorum.

Treatment of Disorderly Deportment

In all instances of irregular and disorderly deportment, it is competent for every member, and is the special duty of the presiding officer, to complain to the assembly, or to take notice of the offence, and call the attention of the assembly to it. When a complaint of this kind is made by the presiding officer, he is said to *name* the member offending; that is, he declares to the assembly, that such a member, calling him by name, is guilty of certain irregular or improper conduct. The presiding officer states the offence committed, and the assembly proceeds to consider the degree and amount of punishment to be inflicted. The assembly may allow the member complained of to remain, when he offers to withdraw; or, on the other hand, it may require him to withdraw, if he does not offer to do so of his own accord. The proceedings are similar when the complaint is made by a member, except that the offence is stated by such member, instead of being stated by the presiding officer.

When Disorderly Member Is Debarred from Assembly

No member ought to be present in the assembly when any matter or business concerning himself is

debating; nor, if present by the indulgence of the
assembly, ought he to vote on any such question.
Whether the matter in question concern his private
interest, or relate to his conduct as a member—as for
a breach of order or for matter arising in debate—as
soon as it is fairly before the assembly the member is
to be heard in exculpation, and then to withdraw until
the matter is settled. If, notwithstanding, a member
should remain in the assembly and vote, his vote may
and ought to be disallowed; it being contrary, not only
to the laws of decency, but to the fundamental principle of the social compact, that a man should sit and
act as a judge in his own case.

Penalties Imposed upon Disorderly Members

The only punishments, which can be inflicted upon
its members by a deliberative assembly of the kind now
under consideration, consist of reprimanding—exclu-
sion from the assembly—a prohibition to speak or vote,
for a specified time—and expulsion. To these are
added such other forms of punishment, as by apology,
begging pardon, etc., as the assembly may see fit to
impose, and to require the offender to submit to, on
pain of expulsion.

CHAPTER IV

Introduction of Business

Setting Business in Motion

The proceedings of a deliberative assembly, in reference to any particular subject, are ordinarily set in motion, in the first instance, by some one of the members either presenting a communication from persons not members, or himself submitting a proposition to the assembly.

Communications

Communications made to the assembly are of two kinds, namely, those which are merely for its information in matters of fact, and those which contain a request for some action on the part of the assembly, either of a general nature or for the benefit of an individual. The latter only, as they alone constitute a foundation for future proceedings, require to be noticed.

Motions[1]

Rules Governing Motions

Rules governing motions in the order of their precedance, or rank, beginning with the motion: "(a) To Fix Time to which to Adjourn," which ranks the highest; and ending with "(m) Main Motion," which ranks lowest.

[1] Note handy motions chart on P. 1.

Signs Representing Governing Rules

* = May interrupt speaker.
† = Does not require a second.
§ = Not debatable.
‖ = Debate limited.
⅔ = Requires a ⅔ vote.

Privileged Motions

(a) Fix Time to Which to Adjourn, ‖.
(b) Adjourn (Unqualified), §.
(c) Take a Recess, ‖.
(d) Rise to a Question of Privilege, *–†–§.
(e) Call for Orders of the Day, *–†–§.

Subsidiary Motions

(f) Lay on, or Take from Table, §.
(g) Call for the Previous Question, §–⅔.
(h) Limit, or Extend Limits, of Debate, ‖–⅔.
(i) Postpone Definitely, ‖.
(j) Refer to a Committee, ‖.
(k) Amend.
(l) Postpone Indefinitely.

Main Motions

(m1) General Main Motion, and (m2) Specific Main Motions:

Take from Table, §. Reconsider, *. Reconsider and Have Entered on Minutes, *–§. Rescind, ⅔. Expunge, ⅔. Adopt a Resolution. Adjourn (Qualified). Create Orders of the Day (Special), ⅔. Amend (Constitution, etc.), ⅔.

Incidental Motions

Suspend Rules, §–⅔. Withdraw a Motion, †–§. Read Papers, §. Object to Consideration, *–†–§–⅔. Rise to a Point of Order, *–†–§. Rise to a Parliamentary Inquiry, *–†–§. Appeal from the Decision of the Chair, *–‖. Call for a Division of the House, *–†–§. Call for a Division of a Question, §.

The motions above listed, beginning at the letter (*a*) and ending at the letter (*m*), all have a definite order of precedence; but the incidental motions have no order of precedence within their own category.

The Rules governing each motion, as indicated by the signs, refer only to the differences between the rules which govern that motion and those which govern the main motion; and the absence of any more signs following the title of any motion indicates that the other rules governing that motion are the same as those governing a main motion.

The principal rules governing a main motion are:

1. A speaker may not be interrupted.
2. Requires a second.
3. May be debated.
4. Majority vote required for its adoption.
5. Motion may be renewed at next session.
6. All motions may apply.

For example, the motion, **"Call for the Previous Question,"** is followed by two signs, *viz.*, § and ⅔, signifying respectively, "undebatable," and, "⅔ vote required to carry." In other respects the motion is governed by the same rules as a main motion, *i.e.*, *"Speaker may not be interrupted,"* and, *"Requires a second, etc."*

Motions, What They Are

Propositions made by members are drawn up and introduced, by motion,* in the form which they are intended by the mover to bear, as orders, resolutions, or votes, if they should be adopted by the assembly. These propositions, of whatever nature they may be, are usually denominated motions, until they are adopted; they then take the name which properly belongs to them.

How to Obtain the Floor

When a member has occasion to make any communication whatever to the assembly—whether to pre-

* See Salient Features of Various Motions, page 97.

sent a petition or other paper, or to make or second a motion of any kind, or merely to make a verbal statement—as well as when one desires to address the assembly in debate, he must ask recognition for the purpose he has in view. In order to do this he must rise in his place,* and address himself to the presiding officer by title. The latter, on hearing himself thus addressed, calls to the member by his name, and the member may then, but not before, proceed with his business.

Floor Given to First Claimant

If two or more members rise and address themselves to the presiding officer at the same time, or nearly so, he should give the floor to the member whose voice was first heard. If his decision should not be satisfactory, any member may call it in question, saying that in his opinion such a member (not the one named) was first up and to have the sense of the assembly taken thereon as to which of the members should be heard. In this case the question should be first taken upon the name of the member announced by the presiding officer; and, if this question should be decided in the negative, then upon the name of the member for whom the floor was claimed in opposition to him.

Communications from Non-members

The mode of proceeding upon such communications from persons not members as are above alluded to may be explained by that adopted on the presentation of a petition, which may be considered as the representative of the whole class to which it belongs.

Petition

A petition, in order to be received, should be subscribed by the petitioner himself, with his own hand,

* In the House of Representatives of Massachusetts, where each member's seat is regularly assigned to him, and numbered, it has been found useful, in deciding upon the claims of several competitors for the floor, to prefer one who rises in his place, to a member who addresses the speaker from the area, the passageways, or the seat of any other member.

either by name or mark, except in case of inability
from sickness, or because the petitioner is attending in
person. It should be presented or offered, not by the
petitioner himself, but by some member to whom it
is intrusted for that purpose.

Petition—Statement of Its Substance

The member who presents a petition should previously have informed himself of its contents, so as to
be able to state the substance of it on offering it to
the assembly, and also to be prepared to say, if any
question should be made, that in his judgment it is
couched in proper language, and contains nothing
intentionally disrespectful to the assembly.

Petition—How to Present It

Being thus prepared, the member rises in his place,
with the petition in his hand, and informs the assembly that he has a certain petition. He states the substance of it, which he thereupon presents or offers to
the assembly, and at the same time moves (which, however, may be done by any other member) that it be
received. This motion being seconded, the question is
put whether the assembly will receive the petition or
not. This is the regular course of proceeding, but in
practice there is seldom any question made on receiving a petition; the presiding officer usually taking it
for granted that there is no objection to the reception,
unless it be stated. If, however, any objection is made
to a petition, before it has been otherwise disposed of,
the presiding officer ought to retrace his steps and
require a motion of reception to be regularly made
and seconded.

Petition—Action On

If the question of reception is determined in the
affirmative, the petition is brought to the table by
the member presenting it; and is there read as of

course by the clerk. It is then regularly before the
assembly, to be dealt with as it thinks proper. The
usual course is either to proceed to consider the subject of it immediately, or to assign some future time
for its consideration, or to order it to lie on the table
for the examination and consideration of the members individually.

Submitting Motions in Writing

A motion must be submitted in writing; otherwise
the presiding officer will be justified in refusing to
receive it. He may do so, however, if he pleases, and is
willing to take the trouble himself to reduce it to
writing. This rule extends only to principal motions,
which, when adopted, become the act and express the
sense of the assembly. It does not extend to subsidiary
or incidental motions* which merely enable the assembly to dispose of the former in the manner it desires,
and which are always in the same form. In the case
of a motion to amend, which is a subsidiary motion,
the rule admits of an exception, so far as regards the
insertion of additional words, which, as well as the
principal motion, must be in writing.

Motions Must Be Seconded

A motion must be seconded, that is, approved by
some one member, at least expressing his approval by
rising and saying that he seconds the motion. If a
motion is not seconded, no notice whatever is to be
taken of it by the presiding officer. Although in practice, very many motions, particularly those which occur in the ordinary routine of business, are admitted
without being seconded. This rule applies as well to
subsidiary as principal motions. The seconding of a
motion seems to be required, on the ground that the
time of the assembly ought not to be taken up by a
question which, for anything that appears, has no one
in its favor but the mover. There are some apparent

---

* Such as, to adjourn—lie on the table—for the previous question
—for postponement—commitment, etc.

exceptions to this rule. In those cases in which one member alone has the right of instituting or giving direction to a particular proceeding; and an actual exception is sometimes made by a special rule, requiring certain motions to be seconded by more than one member.

Motion to Be Stated by Presiding Officer

When a motion has been made and seconded, it is then to be stated by the presiding officer to the assembly, and thus becomes a question for its decision. Until so stated, it is not in order for any other motion to be made, or for any member to speak to it. But, when moved, seconded, and stated from the chair, a motion is in the possession of the assembly, and cannot be withdrawn by the mover, but by special leave of the assembly, which must be obtained by a motion made and seconded as in other cases.

This rule, however, has in recent practice been modified in congressional proceedings to better facilitate the dispatching of business in the two houses. The rule in the Senate now reads: "Any motion or resolution may be withdrawn or modified by the mover at any time before a decision, amendment, or ordering of the yeas and nays, except a motion to reconsider, which shall not be withdrawn without leave of the Senate."

The rule in the House reads: "A motion may be withdrawn at any time before a decision or amendment; but not after an amendment, or any minor decision has been made on it, unless the mover of the motion obtains the consent of the majority, conceded in the usual manner."

When a Motion Is Debatable

When a motion is regularly before the assembly, it is the duty of the presiding officer to state it, if it be not in writing, or to cause it to be read, if it be, as often as any member desires to have it stated or read for his information.

Precedence of a Pending Motion

No other motion is in order when another one, or any proposition, is before the assembly, but if a motion be one referring to a matter which is previous in character to the question then being considered such motion is entitled to precedence.

CHAPTER V

Motions in General

Subsidiary Motions

When a proposition is made to a deliberative assembly, for its adoption, the proposition may be in such form as to be put to the question, and the assembly may be in such a state as to come to a decision upon it at once; and when this is the case nothing more can be necessary than to take the votes of the members and ascertain the result. But a different state of things may, and ordinarily does, exist, and the assembly may prefer some other course of proceeding to an immediate decision of the question in the form in which it is presented; and, as it is proper that every parliamentary body should have the means of fitly disposing of every proposition which may be made to it, certain forms of question have from time to time been invented, and are now in general use, for that purpose. These forms of question may properly be called *subsidiary,* in order to distinguish them from the principal motion or question to which they relate.

Different Kinds of Subsidiary Motions

The different states of mind, in which a proposition may be received by a deliberative assembly, and the corresponding forms of proceeding, or subsidiary motions, to which they give rise, in order to ascertain the sense of the assembly, are the following:

First. The assembly may look upon the proposition as useless or inexpedient; and may therefore desire to suppress it, either for a time, or altogether. The subsidiary motions for this purpose, are the previous question, and indefinite postponement.

Second. The assembly may be willing to entertain and consider a proposition, but not at the time when it is made; either because more information is wanted by the members individually; or because they desire further time for reflection and examination; or because the assembly is then occupied with some other matter, which has more pressing claims upon its present attention. The usual motions, under such circumstances, are postponement to some future day or time, and to lie on the table.

Third. The subject-matter of a proposition may be regarded with favor, but the form in which it is introduced may be so defective, that a more careful and deliberate consideration, than can conveniently be given to it in the assembly itself, may be necessary to put it into a satisfactory form. In this case, it is most proper to refer the proposition to a committee.

Fourth. The proposition may be acceptable, and the form in which it is presented so far satisfactory, that the assembly may be willing to consider and act upon it, with such alterations and amendments as may be thought proper. The motion adapted to this case is to amend.

Other Kinds of Subsidiary Motions

It is not to be supposed that the subsidiary motions above specified are the only ones that have at any time been adopted or used, or that it is not competent for a deliberative assembly to frame new motions at pleasure; but these are the forms in most common use, and are entirely sufficient for all practical purposes.* Neither is it to be supposed that these motions are always applied strictly to the cases to which they most

---

* It is usual, in legislative assemblies, to specify the particular motions that are to be used, and the order in which they may be made. Thus, the rule in the House of Representatives of Congress is, that "when a question is under debate, no motion shall be received but to adjourn, to lie on the table, for the previous question, to postpone to a certain day, to commit, to amend, to postpone indefinitely, which several motions shall have precedence in the order in which they are arranged."

appropriately belong. Several of them are frequently used to effect purposes for which others would be more proper. The misapplications will be taken notice of under the heads of the several motions.

CHAPTER VI

Motions to Suppress

Previous Question and Indefinite Postponement

When a proposition is moved which it is supposed may be regarded by the assembly as useless and inexpedient, and which it may therefore be desirous to get rid of, such proposition may be suppressed for a time by means of the previous question, or altogether by a motion for indefinite postponement.

Previous Question—Use of Previous Question

The original and proper parliamentary use of the previous question, being, as above stated, the suppression of a main question, it seems proper to consider it as one of the subsidiary motions for that purpose; although in this country it has been perverted to a wholly different use, namely, the suppression of debate. This consideration, in connection with the difficulty of the subject, and the importance of a correct understanding of it, makes it proper to devote more room to the previous question than needs to be given to most of the other subsidiary motions. It will first be considered according to its original use and intention; and, afterwards, as used in this country.

Origin of Previous Question

There are several motions which give rise to questions previous in their nature to other questions to which they relate; but the term *previous* has been applied exclusively to a motion denominated the *previous question*, which has for its object the suppression of a principal motion or question. This motion was introduced into the House of Commons in England more than two centuries ago, for the purpose of suppressing subjects of a delicate nature relating to high personages, or the discussion of which might call forth observations of an injurious tendency. When first made use of, the form of motion was, *Shall the main question be put?* and the effect of a decision of it in the negative was to suppress the main question for the whole session. The form of it was afterwards changed to that which it has at present, namely, *Shall the main question be now put?* and the effect of a negative decision of it now is to suppress the main question for the residue of the day only. The operation of this motion in suppressing the question to which it is applied results from the principle that no further consideration or discussion can regularly be had of a subject which it has been decided shall not be put to the question. Therefore, when on the motion of the previous question it has been decided that the principal question shall not now be put, that question is disposed of for the day, and cannot be renewed until the next or some succeeding day. This is the purpose for which the previous question was originally invented, and for which it is still used in the British Parliament.

Effect of Deciding Previous Question in the Negative

But the previous question may be decided in the affirmative as well as the negative, that is, that the main question shall now be put; in which case, that question is to be put immediately, without any further debate, and in the form in which it then exists. This operation of the previous question, when decided affirmatively, has led to the use of it for the purpose of suppressing debate on a principal question, and coming to a vote upon it immediately. This is ordinarily the only object of the previous question as made use of in the legislative assemblies of the United

States.* The operation of a negative decision is different in different assemblies. In some, as, for example, in the House of Representatives of Congress, it operates to dispose of the principal or main question by suppressing or removing it from before the house for the day. In others, as in the House of Representatives of Massachusetts, and in the House of Assembly of New York (in the former by usage only, and in the latter by a rule), the effect of a negative decision of the previous question is to leave the main question under debate for the residue of the sitting, unless sooner disposed of by taking the question, or in some other manner.

Previous Question as Used in England

In England the previous question is used only for suppressing a main question; the object of the mover is to obtain a decision of it in the negative; and the effect of such a decision, though in strictness only to suppress the question for the day, is, practically and by parliamentary usage, to dispose of the subject altogether. In this country the previous question is used chiefly for suppressing debate on a main question; the object of the mover is to obtain a decision of it in the affirmative; and the effect of a decision the other way, though in some assemblies operating technically to suppress the main question for the day only, is, in general, merely to suspend the taking of the question for the day; either leaving the debate to go on during the remainder of the day, or the subject to be renewed on the next or some other day. The operation of an affirmative decision is the same in both countries, *i. e.*, the putting of the main question immediately and without further debate, delay, or consideration.

---

* Mr. Jefferson (Manual, § xxxiv) considers this extension of the previous question as an abuse. He is of opinion that ''its uses would be as well answered by other more simple parliamentary forms, and therefore it should not be favored, but restricted within as narrow limits as possible.'' Notwithstanding this suggestion, however, the use of the previous question, as above stated, has become so firmly established, that it cannot now be disturbed or unsettled.

Indefinite Postponement

Motion for Indefinite Postponement

In order to suppress a question altogether, without coming to a direct vote upon it, in such a manner that it cannot be renewed, the proper motion is for indefinite postponement; that is, a postponement or adjournment of the question, without fixing any date for resuming it. The effect of this motion, if decided in the affirmative, is to quash the proposition entirely; as an indefinite adjournment is equivalent to a dissolution, or the continuance of a suit without day is a discontinuance of it. A negative decision has no effect whatever.

Only when the main question, either in its original or amended form, is pending can this motion be made. It cannot be made while any other motion is pending. When the features of the main question are open on this motion for consideration, its usefulness for closing debate is inferior to a motion "that the question lie on the table." No amendment can be made to a motion to postpone indefinitely.

CHAPTER VII

Motions to Postpone

Motions to Postpone and Lay on Table

If the assembly is willing to entertain and consider a question, but not at the time when it is moved, the proper course is either to postpone the subject to another day, or to order it to lie on the table.

Postponement to a Future Day

When the members individually want more information than they possess at the time a question is moved, or desire further time for reflection and examination, the proper motion is, to postpone the subject to such future day as will answer the views of the assembly.

Improper Use of Motion to Postpone

This motion is sometimes used improperly to get rid of a proposition altogether, as would be done by an indefinite postponement. This is effected by fixing upon a day, which, according to the common course of things, will not arrive until after the assembly has been brought to a close. But a motion worded in this manner is precisely equivalent to a motion for indefinite postponement, and should be so considered and treated. During the pendency of a motion to amend, commit, or postpone indefinitely, a motion to postpone to a certain time can be made.

It is subject to amendment, and the previous question may be applied to it without affecting any other motion that may be pending. The time for postponing must not be beyond the life of that particular legislative body. Debate on this motion must be limited to such explanations as are needful for the members to judge the propriety of passing it.

Motion to Lay on Table

If the assembly has something else before it which claims its present attention, and is therefore desirous to postpone a particular proposition until that subject is disposed of, such postponement may be effected by means of a motion that the matter in question lie on the table. If this motion prevails, the subject so disposed of may be taken up at any time afterwards, and considered, when it may suit the convenience of the assembly.

Other Uses of Motion to Lay on Table

This motion is also sometimes made use of for the final disposition of a subject; and it always has that effect, when no motion is afterwards made to take it up.

CHAPTER VIII

Motions to Commit

Motion to Commit

The third case for the use of a subsidiary motion, as already stated, occurs when the subject-matter of a proposition is regarded with favor, but the form in which it is introduced is so defective that a more careful and deliberate consideration is necessary than can conveniently be given to it in the assembly itself, in order to put it into a satisfactory form. The course of proceeding is then to refer the subject to a committee, which is called a commitment, or, if the subject has already been in the hands of a committee, a recommitment.

Referring of Motions to Standing Committee

If there is a standing committee of the assembly, whose functions embrace the subject in question, the motion should be to refer it to that committee; if there is no such committee, then the motion should be to refer to a select committee. If it is a matter of doubt, whether a particular standing committee is appropriate or not, and propositions are made for a reference to that committee, and also for a reference to a select committee, the former proposition should be first put to the question.

Motion May Be Without Instructions

When a subject is referred or recommitted, the committee may be instructed or ordered by the assembly, as to any part or the whole of the duties assigned them; or the subject may be left with them without instructions. In the former case, the instructions must be obeyed, of course. In the latter, the

committee have full power over the matter, and may
report upon it in any manner they please, provided
they keep within the recognized forms of parliamentary proceedings.

Part of a Subject May Be Committed

A part only of a subject may be committed, without
the residue; or different parts may be committed to
different committees.

Commitment of Motion with Instructions

A commitment with instructions is sometimes made
use of as a convenient mode of procuring information,
and, at the same time, of postponing the consideration
of a subject to a future though uncertain day.

CHAPTER IX

Motions to Amend

Motion to Amend

The last case, for the introduction of subsidiary motions, is when the assembly is satisfied with the subject matter of a proposition, but not with the form of it, or with all its different parts, or desires to make some addition to it. The course of proceeding then is to bring the proposition into the proper form and make its details satisfactory by means of amendments, or of certain proceedings of a similar character and having the same general purpose in view. The latter will be first considered.

Division of Question

Motion to Divide a Motion

When a proposition or motion is complicated, that is, composed of two or more parts, which are so far independent of each other as to be susceptible of division into several questions, and it is supposed that the assembly may approve of some but not of all these parts, it is a compendious mode of amendment to divide the motion into separate questions, to be separately voted upon and decided by the assembly. This division may take place by the order of the assembly, on a motion regularly made and seconded for the purpose.

Divided Motions Become
Independent Propositions

When a motion is thus divided, it becomes a series of questions, to be considered and treated each by itself, as an independent proposition, in the order in which they stand. When they have all been gone through with and decided, the result will be the same as if motions to amend by striking out the several parts had been made and put to the question.

Individual Member Cannot
Have a Question Divided

It is sometimes asserted that it is the right of every individual member to have a complicated question (provided it is susceptible of division) divided into its several parts, and a question put separately on each, on his mere demand, and without any motion or any vote of the assembly for that purpose. But this is a mistake; there is no such rule of parliamentary proceeding. A complicated question can only be separated by moving amendments to it in the usual manner, or by moving for a division of it in the manner above stated.

Rule Governing the Division of a Question

It is not unusual, however, for a deliberative assembly to have a rule providing for the division of a complicated question (provided it is susceptible of division) into its several parts upon the demand of a member. When this is the case, it is for the presiding officer (subject, of course, to the revision of the assembly) to decide, when the division of a motion is demanded, first, whether the proposition is susceptible of division, and, secondly, into how many and what parts it may be divided.

Proposition That Is Divisible

A proposition in order to be divisible must comprehend points so distinct and entire that, if one or more of them be taken away, the others may stand entire and by themselves. However, a qualifying paragraph, as, for example, an exception or a proviso, if separated from the general assertion or statement to which it belongs, does not contain an entire point or proposition.

Filling Blanks

Proposition Containing Blanks

It often happens that a proposition is introduced with blanks purposely left by the mover to be filled by the assembly, either with times and numbers, or with provisions analogous to those of the proposition itself. In the latter case, blanks are filled in the same way, that other amendments by the insertions of words are made. In the former, propositions to fill blanks are not considered as amendments to the question, but as original motions, to be made and decided before the principal question.

Motions to Fill Blanks

When a blank is left to be filled with a time or number, motions may be made for that purpose, and the question taken on each by itself, and before another is made; or several motions may be made and pending before any of them are put to the question. This last mode of proceeding, which is the most usual as well as convenient, requires that the several propositions should be arranged, and the question taken on them, in such order as will the soonest and with the most certainty enable the assembly to come to an agreement.

Order of Filling Blanks

In determining upon the order to be adopted, the object is not to begin at that extreme, which and more being within every man's wish, no one can vote against it, and, yet, if it should be carried in the affirmative, every question for more would be precluded; but, at that extreme, which will be likely to unite the fewest, and then to advance or recede until a number or time is reached which will unite a majority.

When Different Propositions Are Made for Filling Blanks

Hence, when several different propositions are made for filling blanks with a time or number, the rule is that if the *larger* comprehends the *lesser*, as in a question to what day a postponement shall take place—the number of which a committee shall consist—the amount of fine to be imposed—the term and imprisonment—the term of irredeemability of a loan—or the *terminus in quem* in any other case, the question must begin *a maximo*, and be first taken upon the greatest or farthest, and so on to the least or nearest, until the assembly comes to a vote. But, if the *lesser* includes the *greater*, as in questions on the limitation of the rate of interest—on the amount of a tax—on what day the session of a legislative assembly shall be closed by adjournment—on what day the next session shall commence—or the *terminus a quo* in any other case, the question must begin *a minimo*, and be first taken on the least or nearest, and so on to the greatest or most remote, until the assembly comes to a vote.*

Addition, Separation, Transposition

Embodying Two Propositions in One

When the matters contained in two separate propositions might be better put into one, the mode of proceeding is to reject one of them, and then to incorpo-

* In the Senate of the United States the rule is, that in filling blanks, the *largest* sum and *longest* time shall be first put. In the House of Commons, in England, the rule established by usage is, that the *smallest* sum and the *longest* time shall be first put.

rate the substance of it with the other by way of amendment. A better mode, however, if the business of the assembly will admit of its being adopted, is to refer both propositions to a committee, with instructions to incorporate them together in one.

Distributing One Proposition into Two

So, on the other hand, if the matter of one proposition would be more properly distributed into two, any part of it may be struck out by way of amendment, and put into the form of a new and distinct proposition. But in this, as in the former case, a better mode would generally be to refer the subject to a committee.

Transposing

In like manner, if a paragraph or section requires to be transposed, a question must be put on striking it out where it stands, and another for inserting it in the place desired.

Numbering of Sections

The numbers prefixed to the several sections, paragraphs or resolutions which constitute a proposition are merely marginal indications, and no part of the text of the proposition itself. If necessary, they may be altered or regulated by the clerk, without any vote or order of the assembly.

Modification of Amendments by the Mover

Motion to Modify

The mover of a proposition is sometimes allowed to modify it after it has been stated as a question by the presiding officer. However, as this is equivalent to a withdrawal of the motion, in order to substitute another in its place; and, since, as has already been seen, a motion regularly made, seconded, and proposed, cannot be withdrawn without leave; it is clear that the practice alluded to rests only upon general consent. Moreover, if it is objected to, the mover of a proposition must obtain the permission of the assembly, by a motion and question, for the purpose, in order to enable him to modify his proposition.

When an Amendment Has Been Accepted

So, too, when an amendment has been regularly moved and seconded, it is sometimes the practice for the mover of the proposition to which it relates to signify his consent to it, and for the amendment to be thereupon made, without any question being taken upon it by the assembly. As this proceeding, however, is essentially the same with that described in the preceding paragraph, it, of course, rests upon the same foundation, and is subject to the same rule.

General Rules Relating to Amendments

Several Forms of Amendment

All amendments, of which a proposition is susceptible, so far as form is concerned, may be effected in one of three ways, namely: either by inserting or adding certain words; or by striking out certain words; or by striking out certain words and inserting or adding others. These several forms of amendment are subject to certain general rules, which, being equally applicable to them all, require to be stated beforehand.

Natural Order of Amending

When a proposition consists of several sections, paragraphs, or resolutions, the natural order of considering and amending it is to begin at the beginning, and to proceed through it in course by paragraphs; and when a latter part has been amended, it is not in order to recur back and make any alteration or amendment of a former part.

Limiting Amendments

Every amendment which can be proposed, whether by striking out, or inserting, or striking out and inserting, is itself susceptible of amendment, but there can be no amendment of an amendment, to an amendment. This would be such a piling of questions one upon another, as would lead to great embarrassment; and as the line must be drawn somewhere, it has been fixed by usage after the amendment to the amendment. The object, which is proposed to be effected by such a proceeding, must be sought by rejecting the amendment to the amendment, in the form in which it is proposed, and then moving it again in the form in which it is wished to be amended, in which it is only an amendment to an amendment. In order to accomplish this, he who desires to amend an amendment should give notice that, if rejected, in the form in which it is presented, he shall move it again in the form in which he desires to have it adopted.

Explanation of Rule Next Above

Thus, if a proposition consists of A B, and it is proposed to amend by inserting C D, it may be moved to amend the amendment by inserting E F, but it cannot be moved to amend this amendment, as, for example, by inserting G. The only mode by which this can be reached is to reject the amendment in the form in which it is presented, *i. e.*, to insert E F and to move it in the form in which it is desired to be amended, *i. e.*, to insert E F G.

Not Permissible to Amend
Agreement of Assembly

Whatever is agreed to by the assembly, on a vote, either adopting or rejecting a proposed amendment, cannot be afterwards altered or amended.

Explanation of Rule Next Above

Thus, if a proposition consists of A B, and it is moved to insert C; if the amendment prevail, C cannot be afterwards amended, because it has been agreed to in that form; and so, if it is moved to strike out B, and the amendment is rejected, B cannot afterwards be amended, because a vote against striking it out is equivalent to a vote agreeing to it as it stands.

Subject Disagreed upon
Cannot Be Moved Again

Whatever is disagreed to by the assembly, on a vote, cannot be afterwards moved again. This rule is the converse of the preceding, and may be illustrated in the same manner.

Explanation of Rule Next Above

Thus if it is moved to amend A B by inserting C, and the amendment is rejected, C cannot be moved again; or, if it is moved to amend A B by striking out B, and the amendment prevails, B cannot be restored; because, in the first case, C, and, in the other, B, have been disagreed to by a vote.

Incompatibility

The inconsistency or incompatibility of a proposed amendment with one which has already been adopted, is a fit ground for its rejection by the assembly, but not for the suppression of it by the presiding officer, as against order; for, if questions of this nature were allowed to be brought within the jurisdiction of the presiding officer, as matters of order, he might usurp a negative on important modifications, and suppress or embarrass instead of subserving the will of the assembly.

Amendments by Striking Out

Striking Out Paragraphs or Words, etc.

If an amendment is proposed by striking out a particular paragraph or certain words, and the amendment is rejected, it cannot be again moved to strike out the same words or part of them. However, it may be moved to strike out the same words with others, provided the coherence to be struck out be so substantial as to make these, in fact, different propositions from the former.

Explanation of Rule Next Above

Thus, if a proposition consist of A B C D, and it is moved to strike out B C, if this amendment is rejected it cannot be moved again; but it may be moved to strike out A B, or A B C, or B C D, or C D.

Striking Out Amendment Agreed Upon

If an amendment by striking out is agreed to, it cannot be afterwards moved to insert the same words struck out, or a part of them; but it may be moved to insert the same words with others, or a part of the same words with others, provided the coherence to be inserted makes these propositions substantially different from the first.

Explanation of Rule Next Above

Thus, if the proposition A B C D is amended by striking out B C, it cannot be moved to insert B C again; but it may be moved to insert B C with other words, or B with others, or C with others.

Method of Amending a Motion to Strike Out

When it is proposed to amend by striking out a particular paragraph, it may be moved to amend this amendment in three different ways, for instance: if it is moved to amend the proposition A B C D, striking out B C, it may be moved to amend this amendment by striking out B only or C only, or by inserting E, or by striking out B or C, and inserting E.

When Motion to Strike Out Is Pending How the Motion to Retain Amended Paragraph Must Be Made

In the case of a proposed amendment by striking out, the effect of voting upon it, whether it be decided in the affirmative or negative, renders it necessary for those who desire to retain the paragraph to amend it, if any amendment is necessary, before the vote is taken on striking out; as, if struck out, it cannot be restored, and if retained, it cannot be amended.

Precedence of Motions to Amend

As an amendment must necessarily be put to the question before the principal motion, so the question must be put on an amendment to an amendment before it is put on the amendment. However, as this is the extreme limit to which motions may be put upon one another, there can be no precedence of one over another among amendments to amendments. Consequently, they can only be moved one at a time, or, at all events, must be put to the question in the order in which they are moved.

Form of Motions for Striking Out

When a motion for striking out words is put to the question, the parliamentary form always is, whether the words *shall stand as part* of the principal motion, and not whether they *shall be struck out*. The reason for this form of stating the question probably is, that the question may be taken in the same manner on a part as on the whole of the principal motion; which would not be the case if the question was stated on striking out; inasmuch as the question on the principal motion, when it comes to be stated, will be on agreeing to it, and not striking out or rejecting it. Besides, as an equal division of the assembly would produce a different decision of the question, according to the manner of stating it, it might happen, if the question on the amendment was stated on striking out, that the same question would be decided both affirmatively and negatively by the same vote.*

Manner of Stating Motion to Strike Out

On motion to amend by striking out certain words, the manner of stating the question is, first to read the passage proposed to be amended as it stands; then the words proposed to be struck out; and, lastly, the whole passage as it will stand if the amendment is adopted.

Amendments by Inserting

Insertion of Rejected Amendment

If an amendment is proposed by inserting or adding a paragraph or words, and the amendment is rejected, it cannot be moved again to insert the same words or a part of them; but it may be moved to insert the same words with others, or a part of the same words with others, provided the coherence really makes them different propositions.

Explanation of Rule Next Above

Thus, if it is moved to amend the proposition A B by inserting C D, and the amendment is rejected, C D cannot be again moved, but it may be moved to insert C E, or D E, or C D E.

* The common mode of stating the question in the legislative assemblies of this country is on "striking out."

When Proposal to Amend Stands

If it is proposed to amend by inserting a paragraph, and the amendment prevails, it cannot be afterwards moved to strike out the same words or a part of them; but it may be moved to strike out the same words with others,* or a part of the same words with others, provided the coherence be such as to make these propositions really different from the first.

Explanation of Rule Next Above

Thus, if in the example above supposed, the amendment prevails, and C D is inserted it cannot be afterwards moved to strike out C D, but it may be moved to strike out A C, or A C D, or D B, or C D B.

Several Ways to Amend a Proposal to Insert

When it is proposed to amend by inserting a paragraph, this amendment may be amended in three different ways, namely, either by striking out a part of the paragraph; or by inserting something into it; or by striking out and inserting.

Explanation of Rule Next Above

Thus, if it is proposed to amend A B by inserting C D, this amendment may be amended either by striking out C or D, or inserting E, or by striking out C or D and inserting E.

Amending Motion to Insert

When it is proposed to amend by inserting a paragraph, those who are in favor of the amendment should amend it, if necessary, before the question is taken; because if it is rejected, it cannot be moved again, and, if received, it cannot be amended.

* This is the common case of striking out a paragraph, after having amended it by inserting words.

No Precedence in Amendments

There is no precedence of one over another in amendments to amendments by inserting, any more than in amendments to amendments by striking out.

Manner of Stating Question

On a motion to amend by inserting a paragraph, the manner of stating the question is, first, to read the passage to be amended, as it stands; then the words proposed to be inserted; and, lastly, the whole passage as it will stand if the amendment prevails.

Amendments by Striking Out and Inserting

Amending by Striking Out and Inserting

The third form of amending a proposition, namely, by striking out certain words and inserting others in their place, is, in fact, a combination of the other two forms, and may, accordingly, be divided into those two forms either by a vote of the assembly or on the demand of a member, under a special rule to that effect.

When the Motion Is Divided

If the motion is divided, the question is first to be taken on striking out; and if that is decided in the affirmative, then on inserting; but if the former is decided in the negative, the latter falls, of course. On a division the proceedings are the same in reference to each branch of the question, beginning with the striking out, as if each branch had been moved by itself.

When Motion to Strike Out and Insert Is Undivided

If the motion to strike out and insert is put to the question undivided, and is decided in the negative, the same motion cannot be made again; but it may be moved to strike out the same words, and, (1) insert nothing; (2) insert other words; (3) insert the same words with others; (4) insert a part of the same words with others; (5) strike out the same words with others, and insert the same; (6) strike out a part of the same words with others, and insert the same; (7) strike out other words and insert the same; and, (8) insert the same words without striking out anything.

When Motion to Strike Out and Insert Is Decided in the Affirmative

If the motion to strike out and insert is decided in the affirmative, it cannot be then moved to insert the words struck out, or part of them, or to strike out the words inserted, or part of them; but it may be moved, (1) to insert the same words with others; (2) to insert a part of the same words with others; (3) to strike out the same words with others; or (4) to strike out a part of the same words with others.

How to Amend a Motion by Striking Out and Inserting

When it is proposed to amend by striking out and inserting, this amendment may be amended in three different ways in the paragraph proposed to be struck out, and also in the paragraph proposed to be inserted, namely, by striking out, or inserting, or striking out and inserting. And those who are in favor of either paragraph must amend it, before the question is taken, for the reasons already stated, namely, that, if decided in the affirmative, the part struck out cannot be restored, nor can the part inserted be amended; and, if decided in the negative, the part proposed to be struck out cannot be amended, nor can the paragraph proposed to be inserted be moved again.

Manner of Stating Motion to Amend by Striking Out and Inserting

On a motion to amend by striking out certain words and inserting others, the manner of stating the question is first to read the whole passage to be amended, as it stands; then the words proposed to be struck out; and, lastly, the whole passage as it will stand when amended.

Amendments Changing the Nature of a Question

Only Those Friendly to a Proposition Should Amend

The term "amendment" is in strictness applicable only to those changes of a proposition by which it is improved, that is, rendered more effectual for the purpose which it has in view, or made to express more clearly and definitely the sense which it is intended to express. Hence it seems proper that those only should undertake to amend a proposition who are friendly to it; but this is by no means the rule. When a proposition is regularly moved and seconded, it is in the possession of the assembly and cannot be withdrawn but by its leave. It has then became the basis of the future proceedings of the assembly, and may be put into any shape and turned to any purpose that the assembly may think proper.

Allowable to Alter Nature of Proposition by Amendment

It is consequently allowable to amend a proposition in such a manner as entirely to alter its nature, and to make it bear a sense different from what it was originally intended to bear; so that the friends of it, as it was first introduced, may themselves be forced to vote against it in its amended form.

Explanation of Rule Next Above

This mode of proceeding is sometimes adopted for the purpose of defeating a proposition by compelling its original friends to unite with those who are opposed to it in voting for its rejection. Thus, in the British House of Commons, January 29, 1765, a resolution being moved, "That a general warrant for apprehending the authors, printers, or publishers of a libel, together with their papers, is not warranted by law, and is a high violation of the liberty of the subject:"—it was moved to amend this motion by prefixing the following paragraph, namely: "That in the particular case of libels, it is proper and necessary to fix, by a vote of this house only, what ought to be deemed the law in respect of general warrants; and, for that purpose, at the time when the determination of the legality of such warrants, in the instance of a most seditious and treasonable libel, is actually depending before the courts of law, for this house to declare"—*that a general warrant for apprehending the authors, printers, or publishers of a libel, together with their papers, is not warranted by law, and is a high violation of the liberty of the subject*. The amendment was adopted, after a long debate, and then the resolution as amended was immediately rejected without a division.*

---

* This mode of defeating a measure, however, is not always successful. In 1780, Mr. Dunning having made a motion in the House of Commons, "that, in the opinion of this house, the influence of the crown has increased, is increasing, and ought to be diminished," Dundas, lord-advocate of Scotland, in order to defeat the motion, proposed to amend, by inserting after the words, *in the opinion of this house*, the words *it is now necessary to declare that*, etc. But this amendment, instead of intimidating the friends of the original motion, was at once adopted by them, and the resolution passed as amended.

Amending Proposition to Change Its Sense

But sometimes the nature of a proposition is changed by means of amendments, with a view to its adoption, in a sense the very opposite of what it was originally intended to bear. The following is a striking example of this mode of proceeding. In the House of Commons, April 10, 1744, a resolution was moved declaring: "That the issuing and paying to the Duke of Aremberg the sum of forty thousand pounds sterling to put the Austrian troops in motion in 1742 was a dangerous misapplication of public money, and destructive of the rights of parliament." The object of this resolution was to censure the conduct of the ministers; and the friends of the ministry, being in a majority, might have voted directly upon the motion and rejected it. But they preferred to turn it into a resolution approving of the conduct of ministers on the occasion referred to; and it was accordingly moved to amend by leaving out the words "a dangerous misapplication," etc., to the end of the motion, and inserting instead thereof the words "necessary for putting the said troops in motion, and of great consequence to the common cause." The amendment being adopted, it was resolved (reversing the original proposition) "That the issuing and paying to the Duke of Aremberg the sum of forty thousand pounds, to put the Austrian troops in motion in the year 1742, was necessary for putting the said troops in motion, and of great consequence to the common cause."

Mode of Defeating by Amendment

It is a mode of defeating a proposition, somewhat similar to that above mentioned, to carry out or extend the principle of it, by means of amendments, so as to show the inconvenience, absurdity, or danger of its adoption, with such evident clearness, that it becomes impossible for the assembly to agree to it. Thus, a motion having been made in the House of Commons, "for copies of all the letters written by the lords of the admiralty to a certain officer in the navy," it was

moved to amend the motion by adding these words:—
"which letters may contain orders, or be relative
orders, not executed, and still subsisting." This amendment being adopted, the motion as amended was unani-
mously rejected.

Matters in Opposition to Original Proposition Introduced by Amendment

It will be seen, from the foregoing examples, that
as the mover of a proposition is under no restriction
as to embracing incongruous matters under the same
motion, so, on the other hand, the assembly may en-
graft upon a motion, by way of amendment, matter
which is not only incongruous with but entirely opposed to the motion as originally introduced. In legislative assemblies it is not unusual to amend a bill by
striking out all after the enacting clause and inserting
an entirely new bill, or to amend a resolution by striking out all after the words "Resolved that" and inserting a proposition of a wholly different tenor.

CHAPTER X

Order and Succession of Questions

Questions Which May Be Considered Before Main Question*

It is a general rule that when a proposition is before a deliberative assembly for its consideration, no other proposition or motion can regularly be made to arise, so as to take the place of the former, and be first acted upon, unless it be either, *first*, a privileged question; *secondly*, a subsidiary question; or, *thirdly,* an incidental question or motion.

Questions Taking the Place of Main Question

All these motions take the place of the principal motion, or main question, as it is usually called, and are to be first put to the question; and, among themselves, also, there are some, which, in like manner, take the place of all the others. Some of these questions merely supersede the principal question, until they have been decided; and, when decided, whether affirmatively or negatively, leave that question as before. Others of them also supersede the principal question until they are decided; and when decided one way, dispose of the principal question; but if decided the other way leave it as before.

Privileged Questions

Privileged Questions

There are certain motions or questions which, on account of the superior importance attributed to them,

* Note handy motions chart on P. 1.

either in consequence of a vote of the assembly, or in themselves considered, or of the necessity of the proceedings to which they lead, are entitled to take the place of any other subject or proposition which may then be under consideration, and to be first acted upon and decided by the assembly. These are called privileged questions, because they are entitled to precedence over other questions, though they are of different degrees among themselves. Questions of this nature are of three kinds, namely : *first*, motions to adjourn ; *secondly*, motions or questions relating to the rights and privileges of the assembly, or of its members individually ; and, *thirdly*, motions for the orders of the day.

Motion to Adjourn

A motion to adjourn takes the place of all other questions whatsoever*; for, otherwise, the assembly might be kept sitting against its will, and for an indefinite time ; but, in order to entitle this motion to precedence, it must be simply to "adjourn," without the addition of any particular day or time. And, as the object of this motion, when made in the midst of some other proceeding, and with a view to supersede a question already proposed, is simply to break up the sitting, it does not admit of any amendment by the addition of a particular day, or in any other manner. Although, if a motion to adjourn is made, when no other business is before the assembly, it may be amended like other questions.

But in some instances a motion to adjourn may be made, unless a decision by the assembly has been made against it ; or unless a time has already been designated for the presiding officer to declare an adjournment, or when the time and place of the next meeting is

* It is commonly said, that a motion to adjourn is always in order, but this is not precisely true. The question of adjournment may, indeed, be moved repeatedly on the same day ; yet, in strictness, not without some intermediate question being proposed, after one motion to adjourn is disposed of, and before the next motion is made for adjourning; as, for example, an amendment to a pending question, or for the reading of some paper. The reason of this is that, until some other proceeding has intervened, the question already decided is the same as that newly moved.

under consideration, or when a vote is in progress or a member has the floor.

A motion is not debatable when it is made merely to adjourn; but if qualified as to a certain time or *without day*, it could in that case be divided and would be debatable.

Manner of Making a Motion to Adjourn

A motion to adjourn is merely, "that this assembly do now adjourn"; and, if it is carried in the affirmative, the assembly is adjourned to the next sitting day; unless it has previously come to a resolution, that, on rising, it will adjourn to a particular day; in which case it is adjourned to that day. When the question has been put the presiding officer announces whether the "ayes" or "nos" seem to prevail; but should the vote of the whole assembly be obviously one way the chairman is supposed to at once declare an adjournment, and this becomes final.

It has occurred in some instances that a chairman has declined to put a motion where the motion was made and seconded; and a competent court decision in one instance was to the effect that the chairman was not obliged to adjourn the meeting notwithstanding that a majority of the assembly present wanted an adjournment.

The court decided against the contention that any meeting was inherently empowered to determine upon adjournment if it saw fit, and that the duty of the chairman is to put the motion when made and seconded; but maintained that such power was not vested in a body where the articles expressly state under what conditions an adjournment may be taken.

Adjournment Without Day

An adjournment without day,* that is, without any time being fixed for reassembling, would, in the case

---

* It is quite common, when the business of a deliberative assembly has been brought to a close, to adjourn the assembly without day. A better form is to dissolve it; as an adjournment without day, if we regard the etymology of the word adjourn, is a contradiction in terms.

of any other than a legislative assembly, be equivalent to a dissolution.

Adjournment on Pending Question

When a question is interrupted by an adjournment before any vote or question has been taken upon it, it is thereby removed from before the assembly, and will not stand before it, as a matter of course, at its next meeting, but must be brought forward in the usual way.

Questions of Privilege

Nature of the Questions

These questions are such, that although they do not relate to the pending question, are of such importance that they take precedence over all other questions and because of that privilege are not debatable. Excepting the motions to fix the time to which to adjourn and to take a recess which may be amended, no subsidiary motion can be applied to them. But after the assembly has taken up the orders of the day or a question of privilege, debate and amendment are allowed and the subsidiary motions are applicable just as on any main motion.

These privileged motions are: (*a*) Fix the time to which to adjourn (*if made when another question is pending*). (*b*) To adjourn (*without qualifying and will not cause the assembly to dissolve*). (*c*) To take a recess (*if made while another question is pending*). (*d*) Raise a question of privilege. (*e*) Call for orders of the day.

There are some motions which cannot definitely be classified as whether subsidiary, incidental, or privileged; and two main motions. These motions are: (*a*) To take from the table. (*b*) Reconsider. (*c*) Rescind (a main motion). (*d*) Renewal of a motion. (*e*) Ratify (a main motion). (*f*) Dilatory, absurd, or frivolous motions. (*g*) Call of the house.

Orders of the Day

Nature of Orders of the Day

When the consideration of a subject has been assigned for a particular day, by an order of the assembly, the matter so assigned is called the order of the day for that day. If, in the course of business, as commonly happens in legislative assemblies, there are several subjects assigned for the same day, they are called the orders of the day.

Precedence of Orders of the Day

A question, which is thus made the subject of an order for its consideration on a particular day, is thereby made a privileged question for that day; the order being a repeal, as to this special case, of the general rule as to business. If, therefore, any other proposition (with the exception of the two preceding) is moved or arises on the day assigned for the consideration of a particular subject, a motion for the order of the day will supersede the question first made, together with all subsidiary and incidental questions connected with it, and must be put and decided; for if the debate or consideration of that subject were allowed to proceed it might continue through the day, and thus defeat the order.

Motion to Proceed to Orders of the Day Must Be Qualified

But this motion, to entitle it to precedence, must be for the orders generally, if there is more than one, and not for any particular one. If decided in the affirmative, that is, that the assembly will now proceed to the orders of the day, they must then be read and gone through within the order in which they stand; priority of order being considered to give priority of right.

When a Motion to Proceed to Order of the Day Is Privileged

If the consideration of a subject is assigned for a particular hour on the day named, a motion to proceed to it is not a privileged motion until that hour has arrived; but, if no hour is fixed, the order is for the entire day and every part of it.

Proper Time to Take Up Orders

Where there are several orders of the day, and one of them is fixed for a particular hour, if the orders are taken up before that hour, they are to be proceeded with as they stand, until that hour, and then the subject assigned for that hour is the next in order. However, if the orders are taken up at that time or afterwards, that particular subject must be considered as the first in order.

Renewal of Original Question When Motion for Orders Is Decided in Affirmative

If the motion for the orders of the day is decided in the affirmative, the original question is removed from before the assembly, in the same manner as if it had been interrupted by an adjournment, and does not stand before the assembly, as a matter of course, at its next meeting, but must be renewed in the usual way.

When a Decision Is in Negative to Proceed with Orders

If the motion is decided in the negative, the vote of the assembly is a discharge of the orders, so far as they interfere with the consideration of the subject then before it, and entitles that subject to be first disposed of.

Result of Failure to Proceed in Orders

Orders of the day, unless proceeded in and disposed of on the day assigned, fall, of course, and must be renewed for some other day. It may be provided, however, by a special rule, as in the legislative assemblies of Massachusetts, that the orders for a particular day shall hold for every succeeding day until disposed of.

Incidental Questions—Nature of

Incidental questions are such as arise out of other questions, and are consequently to be decided before the questions which give rise to them. Of this nature are, *first,* questions of order; *second,* motions for the reading of papers, etc.; *third,* leave to withdraw a motion; *fourth,* suspension of a rule; and, *fifth,* amendment of an amendment.

Questions of Order

Enforcing Rules and Orders

It is the duty of the presiding officer to enforce the rules and orders of the body over which he presides, in all its proceedings; and this without question, debate, or delay, in all cases, in which the breach of order, or the departure from rule, is manifest. It is also the right of every member taking notice of the breach of a rule, to insist upon the enforcement of it in the same manner.

Questions as to Fact of Breach of Order

But, though no question can be made, as to the enforcement of the rules, when there is a breach or manifest departure from them, so long as any member insists upon their enforcement; yet questions may and do frequently arise, as to the fact of there being a breach of order, or a violation of the rules in a particular proceeding; and these questions must be decided before a case can arise for the enforcement of the rules. Questions of this kind are denominated questions of order.

Question Supersedes Subject from Which It Proceeds

When any question of this nature arises, in the course of any other proceeding, it necessarily supersedes the further consideration of the subject out of which it arises until that question is disposed of. Then the original motion or proceeding revives, and resumes its former position, unless it has itself been disposed of by the question of order.

When a Question of Order Is Raised

When a question of order is raised, as it may be by any one member, it is not stated from the chair and decided by the assembly, like other questions, but is decided, in the first instance, by the presiding officer, without any previous debate or discussion by the assembly. If the decision of the presiding officer is not satisfactory, any one member may object to it, and have the question decided by the assembly. This is called *appealing* from the decision of the chair. The question is then stated by the presiding officer on the appeal, namely: *Shall the decision of the chair stand as the decision of the assembly?* It is thereupon debated and decided by the assembly in the same manner as any other question, except that the presiding officer is allowed to take a part in the debate, which, on ordinary occasions, he is prohibited from doing.

Reading Papers

Right of Members to Have Papers Read

It is, for obvious reasons, a general rule that, where papers are laid before a deliberative assembly, for its action, every member has a right to have them once read at the table, before he can be compelled to vote on them. Consequently, when the reading of any paper, relative to a question before the assembly, is called for under this rule, no question need be made as to the reading. The paper is read by the clerk, under the direction of the presiding officer, as a matter of course.

Members Reading Papers with Leave of Assembly

But, with the exception of papers coming under this rule, it is not the right of any member to read himself, or to have read, any paper, book, or document whatever, without the leave of the assembly, upon a motion made and a question put for the purpose. The delay and interruption, which could otherwise ensue from reading every paper that might be called for, show the absolute necessity of restricting the rule within the narrowest possible limits, consistently with permitting every member to have as much information as possible on the subjects in reference to which he is about to vote.

Obtaining Leave to Read Papers

When, therefore, a member desires that any paper, book, or document, on the table, whether printed or written (except as above mentioned), should be read for his own information, or that of the assembly; or desires to read any such book, paper, or document, in his place, in the course of a debate, or otherwise; or even to read his own speech, which he has prepared beforehand and committed to writing; in all these cases, if any objection is made, he must obtain leave of the assembly for the reading by a motion and vote for the purpose.

Leave to Read Papers Usually Allowed

When the reading of a paper is evidently for information, and not for delay, it is the usual practice for the presiding officer to allow it, unless objection is made, in which case leave must be asked. This is seldom refused where there is no intentional or gross abuse of the time and patience of the assembly.

Members May Insist on Reading

It is not now the practice, as it once was in legislative assemblies, to read all papers that are presented, especially when they are referred to committees immediately on their presentation, though the right of every member to insist upon one reading is still admitted. It would be impossible, with the amount of business done by legislative bodies of the present day, to devote much of their time to the reading of papers.

Precedence of Motion to Read a Paper

When in the course of a debate or other proceeding, the reading of a paper is called for, and a question is made upon it, this question is incidental to the former, and must be first decided.

Withdrawal of a Motion

When a Motion Cannot Be Withdrawn

A motion, when regularly made, seconded, and proposed from the chair, is then in possession of the assembly, and cannot be withdrawn by the mover, or directly disposed of in any manner but by vote. Consequently, if the mover of a question wishes to modify it, or to substitute a different one in its place, he must obtain the leave of the assembly for that purpose. This leave can only be had, if objection is made, by a motion and question in the usual mode of proceeding.

Result of Decision

If this motion is decided in the affirmative, the motion to which it relates is thereby removed from before the assembly, as if it had never been moved; if in the negative, the business proceeds as before.

Suspension of a Rule

When Rule Is Suspended

When any contemplated motion or proceeding is rendered impracticable, by reason of the existence of some special rule by which it is prohibited, it has become an established practice in this country, to suspend or dispense with the rule, for the purpose of admitting the proceeding or motion which is desired. This can only be done by a motion and question. Where this course is taken in order to a motion having reference to a proposition then under consideration, a motion to suspend the rule supersedes the original question for the time being, and is first to be decided.

Provision for Suspension of Rules

It is usual, in the code of rules adopted by deliberative assemblies, and especially legislative bodies, to provide that a certain number exceeding a majority, as two-thirds or three-fourths, shall be competent to the suspension of a rule in a particular case. Where this is not provided, there seems to be no other mode of suspending or dispensing with a rule than by general consent.

Amendment of Amendments

The Amendment to Be Put First

In treating of amendments, it has already been seen that it is allowable to amend a proposed amendment; and that the question on such sub-amendment must necessarily be put and decided before putting the question on the amendment. The former is incidental to the latter, and supersedes it for the time being.

Subsidiary Questions

Nature of

Subsidiary, or secondary, questions or motions, as has already been stated, are those which relate to a principal motion, and are made use of to enable the assembly to dispose of it in the most appropriate manner. These motions have the effect to supersede, and in some cases, when decided one way, to dispose of the principal question. They are also of different degrees among themselves, and, according to their several natures, supersede, and sometimes dispose of, one another.

Designation of

The subsidiary motions in common use are the following, namely: lie on the table—the previous question—postponement, either indefinite or to a certain day—commitment—and amendment.

Subsidiary Motions Cannot Be Applied to One Another

It is a general rule, with certain exceptions which will be immediately mentioned, that subsidiary motions cannot be applied to one another. For example, in the case of a motion to postpone, commit or amend a principal question, it cannot be moved to suppress the motion to postpone, etc., by putting a previous question on it; for, suppose the previous question is moved, or a commitment, or amendment, of a main question, it cannot be moved to postpone the previous question, or the motion for commitment or amendment. The reasons for this rule are: (1) It would be absurd to separate the appendage from its principal; (2) it would be a piling of questions one on another, which, to avoid embarrassment, is not allowed; and (3) the same result may be reached more simply by voting against the motion which it is attempted to dispose of by another secondary motion.

Exceptions to Rule Next Above

The exceptions to the rule above stated are, that motions to postpone (either to a certain day or indefinitely), to commit, or to amend a principal question, may be amended, for the reason that the useful character of amendment gives it a privilege of attaching itself to a secondary and privileged motion; that is, a subsidiary motion to carry out and improve another may be applied to that other, but a subsidiary motion to dispose of or suppress another is not admissible. Hence, the subsidiary motions above mentioned may be amended.

Previous Question Cannot Be Amended

A previous question, however, cannot be amended; the nature of it not admitting of any change. Parliamentary usage has fixed its form to be, Shall the main question be now put? that is, at this instant; and, as the present instant is but one, it cannot admit of any modification; and to change it to the next day or any other moment is without example or utility. For the same reasons, also, that the form of it is fixed by parliamentary usage, and is already as simple as it can be, a motion to lay on the table cannot be amended.

Lay on the Table

When Motion Is Made

This motion is usually resorted to when the assembly has something else before it which claims its present attention, and therefore desires to lay aside a proposition for a short but indefinite time, reserving to itself the power to take it up when convenient. This motion takes precedence of and supersedes all the other subsidiary motions, and becomes the sole question under consideration. In this case, if any debate on any other motion was going on, it is discontinued, and as this motion is not debatable, the question must be decided at once.

Result of Affirmative Decision

If decided in the affirmative, the principal motion, together with all the other motions, subsidiary and incidental, connected with it, is removed from before the assembly, until it is again taken up; which it may be, by motion and vote, at any time, when the assembly pleases.

Result of Negative Decision

If decided in the negative, the business proceeds in the same manner as if the motion had never been made.

Motion to Lay Main Question on Table Subject to Call

When a motion is made to lay main question on table, it is not debatable; but it may be taken up again for consideration when the way is open, and no motion is necessary, the call of any member being sufficient for the purpose.

Previous Question

Standing of Previous Question

This motion has already been described on page 54 and the nature and effect of it fully stated. It stands in an equal degree with all the other subsidiary motions, except the motion to lay on the table; and, consequently, if first moved, is not subject to be superseded by a motion to postpone, commit, or amend.

Effect of Previous Question

If the previous question is moved before the others above mentioned, and put to the question, it has the effect to prevent those motions from being made at all. If the decision is affirmative, to wit, that the main question shall now be put, it would of course be contrary to the decision of the assembly, and therefore against order, to postpone, commit, or amend. If the decision is negative, *i. e.*, that the main question shall not now be put, this takes the main question out of the possession of the assembly for the day, so that there is nothing then before it to postpone, commit, or amend.

Postponement

Motion to Postpone May Be Amended

The amendment to postpone is either indefinite or to a day certain, and in both these forms may be amended; in the former by making it to a certain day, in the latter by substituting one day for another. But, in the latter case, propositions to substitute different days for that originally named bear more resemblance to propositions for filling blanks than they do to amendments, and should be considered and treated accordingly.

Motion to Amend May Be Made to a Certain Day

If, therefore, a motion is made for an indefinite postponement, it may be moved to amend the motion by making it to a certain day. If any other day is desired, it may be moved as an amendment to the amendment; or it may be moved as an independent motion when the amendment has been rejected.

Motion May Be Amended to Postpone to a Certain Day

If a motion is made for a postponement to a certain day it may be amended by the substitution of a different day; but in this case a more simple and effectual mode of proceeding is to consider the day as a blank, to be filled in the usual manner, beginning with the longest time.

Rank of Motion Next Above

This motion stands in the same degree with motions for the previous question—to commit—and to amend; and, if first made, is not susceptible of being superseded by them.

Result of Decision of Motion

If a motion for postponement is decided affirmatively, the proposition to which it is applied is removed from before the assembly, with all its appendages and incidents, and consequently there is no ground for either of the other subsidiary motions. If it is decided negatively that the proposition shall not be postponed, that question may then be suppressed by the previous question or committed, or amended.

Commitment

How to Amend a Motion to Commit

A motion to commit, or recommit (which is the term used when the proposition has already been once committed), may be amended, by the substitution of one kind of committee for another, or by enlarging or diminishing the number of the members of the committee, as originally proposed, or by instructions to the committee.

A motion to commit, resulting from debate with a

view to removing objections or improving, is debatable, as the merits of the bill itself are involved.

Rank of Motion to Commit

This motion stands in the same degree with the previous question and postponement; and, if first made, is not superseded by them, but it takes precedence of a motion to amend.

Result of Decision on Motion Next Above

If decided affirmatively, the proposition is removed from before the assembly; and consequently there is no ground for the previous question, or for the postponement, or amendment. If it is decided negatively, to wit, that the principal question shall not be committed, that question may then be suppressed by the previous question, or postponed, or amended.

Amendment

Rank of Motion to Amend

A motion to amend, as has been seen, may be itself amended. It stands in the same degree only with the previous question and indefinite postponement, and neither, if first moved, is superseded by the other.

Motion to Amend May Be Superseded

But this motion is liable to be superseded by a motion to postpone to a certain day; so that amendment and postponement competing, the latter is to be first put. The reason is, that a question for amendment is not suppressed by postponing or adjourning the principal question, but remains before the assembly, whenever the main question is resumed. Otherwise, it might happen that the occasion for other urgent business might go by and be lost by length of debate on the amendment, if the assembly had no power to postpone the whole subject.

Motion to Amend May Be Superseded by Motion to Commit

A motion to amend may also be superseded by a motion to commit; so that the latter, though subsequently moved, is to be first put; because, "in truth, it facilitates and befriends the motion to amend."

Effect of Decision

The effect of both a negative and an affirmative decision of amendments has already been considered, (pages 67 to 79).

Note—Much advantage may be derived by a careful perusal of, and committing to memory, the following essential and salient features, given in the abstract, of the various motions made in parliamentary procedure.

Of Main Motions

1. A speaker may not be interrupted.
2. Requires a second.
3. Debatable.
4. Majority vote required.
5. Motion may be renewed at next session.
6. All motions may apply.

Of Amendments

1. A speaker may not be interrupted.
2. Requires a second.
3. Debatable.
4. Majority vote required.
5. Motion may not be renewed.
6. Motions that may apply are: Amend—Limit debate—Previous question—Reconsider.

Of Point of Order

1. A speaker may not be interrupted.
2. No second required.

3. Not debatable.
4. If not decided by chairman a majority vote is required.
5. Motion may not be renewed.
6. No motions may apply.

Of Request for Information

1. A speaker may be interrupted.
2. No second required.
3. Not debatable.
4. No vote required.
5. May not be renewed.
6. No motions apply.

Of Previous Question

1. A speaker may not be interrupted.
2. Requires a second.
3. Not debatable.
4. ⅔ vote required.
5. May be renewed after debate.
6. Motion to reconsider may apply.

Of to Limit and Extend Limits of Debate

1. A speaker may not be interrupted.
2. Requires a second.
3. Debate limited.
4. ⅔ vote required.
5. May be renewed after debate.
6. Motions that may apply are: Amend—Reconsider.

Of to Refer to a Committee

1. A speaker may not be interrupted.
2. Requires a second.
3. Debate limited.
4. Majority vote required.
5. May be renewed after debate.
6. Motions that may apply are: Amend—Limit debate—Previous question—Reconsider.

Of Question of Privilege

1. A speaker may be interrupted.
2. No second required.
3. Not debatable.
4. No vote—chairman decides.
5. May be renewed after debate.
6. All motions may apply.

Of Resolutions

1. A speaker may not be interrupted.
2. Requires a second.
3. Motion is debatable.
4. Majority vote required.
5. May be renewed at next session.
6. All motions may apply.

Of Appeal from Decision of Chair

1. A speaker may be interrupted.
2. Requires a second.
3. Debate limited.
4. Majority vote required.
5. May not be renewed.
6. All motions apply except amend.

Of to Lay on Table

1. A speaker may not be interrupted.
2. Requires a second.
3. Not debatable.
4. Majority vote required.
5. May be renewed after debate.
6. No motions apply.

Of to Take from the Table

1. A speaker may not be interrupted.
2. Requires a second.
3. Not debatable.
4. Majority vote required.
5. May be renewed after business has intervened.
6. No motions apply.

Of Postpone Indefinitely

1. A speaker may not be interrupted.
2. Requires a second.
3. Debatable.
4. Majority vote required.
5. May not be renewed.
6. Motions that apply are: Limit debate—Previous question—Reconsider.

Of Postpone Definitely

1. A speaker may not be interrupted.
2. Requires a second.
3. Debate limited.
4. Majority vote required.
5. May be renewed after debate.
6. Motions that may apply are: Amend—Limit debate—Previous question—Reconsider.

Of Create Orders of the Day

1. A speaker may not be interrupted.
2. Requires a second.
3. Debatable.
4. General—majority special ⅔ vote required.
5. May be renewed after debate.
6. All motions apply.

Of Call for Orders of the Day

1. A speaker may be interrupted.
2. No second required.
3. Not debatable.
4. No vote required.
5. May be renewed after business pending is disposed of.
6. No motions may apply.

Of Object to Consideration

1. A speaker may be interrupted.
2. No second required.

3. Not debatable.
4. $\frac{2}{3}$ in negative vote required.
5. May not be renewed.
6. Motion to reconsider may apply.

Of Suspend Rules

1. A speaker may not be interrupted.
2. Requires a second.
3. Not debatable.
4. $\frac{2}{3}$ vote required.
5. May not be renewed except by unanimous consent.
6. No motions apply.

Of Without a Motion

1. A speaker may not be interrupted.
2. No second required.
3. Not debatable.
4. Majority vote required.
5. May be renewed after debate.
6. Motion to reconsider may apply.

Of to Adjourn

1. A speaker may not be interrupted.
2. Requires a second.
3. Not debatable.
4. Majority vote required.
5. May be renewed after debate.
6. No motions apply.

Of Fix Time to Which to Adjourn

1. A speaker may not be interrupted.
2. Requires a second.
3. Limited debate.
4. Majority vote required.
5. May not be renewed for some time.
6. Motions that may apply are: Amend—Reconsider.

Of Take a Recess

1. A speaker may not be interrupted.
2. Requires a second.
3. Debate limited.
4. Majority vote required.
5. May be renewed after business has been disposed of.
6. Motion to amend may apply.

Of Reconsider

1. A speaker may be interrupted.
2. Requires a second.
3. Debatable.
4. Majority vote required.
5. May not be renewed.
6. Motions that may apply are: Limit debate—Previous question—Postpone definitely—Lay on table.

Of Reconsider and Have Entered on the Minutes

1. A speaker may be interrupted.
2. Requires a second.
3. Not debatable.
4. No vote required until called up.
5. May not be renewed.
6. No motions may apply.

Of Rescind

1. A speaker may not be interrupted.
2. Requires a second.
3. Debatable.
4. $\frac{2}{3}$ vote required.
5. May not be renewed.
6. All motions may apply.

Of Expunge

1. A speaker may not be interrupted.
2. Requires a second.

3. Debatable.
4. ⅔ vote required.
5. May not be renewed.
6. All motions may apply.

CHAPTER XI

Order of Proceeding

Presiding Officer Can Exercise Discretion

When several subjects are before the assembly, that is, on their table for consideration (for there can be but a single subject *under* consideration at the same time), and no priority has been given to any one over another, the presiding officer is not precisely bound to any order, as to what matters shall be first taken up; but is left to his own discretion, unless the assembly on a question decide to take up a particular subject.

Settled Order of Business Desirable

A settled order of business, however, where the proceedings of an assembly are likely to last a considerable time, and the matters before it are somewhat numerous, is useful if not necessary for the government of the presiding officer, and to restrain individual members from calling up favorite measures, or matters under their special charge, out of their just time. It is also desirable, for directing the discretion of the assembly, when a motion is made to take up a particular matter, to the prejudice of others, which are of right entitled to be first attended to, in the general order of business.

Method of Establishing the Order

The order of business may be established in virtue of some general rule, or by special orders, relating to each particular subject, and must, of course, necessarily depend upon the nature and amount of the matters before the assembly.

Natural Order

The natural order, in considering and amending any paper which consists of several distinct propositions, is to begin at the beginning and proceed through it by paragraphs. This order of proceeding, if strictly adhered to, as it should always be in numerous assemblies, would prevent any amendment in a former part from being admissible after a latter part had been amended. But this rule does not seem to be so essential to be observed in smaller bodies, in which it may often be advantageous to allow of going from one part of a paper to another, for the purpose of amendments.

One Exception to Natural Order

To this natural order of beginning at the beginning there is one exception, according to parliamentary usage, where a resolution or series of resolutions or other paper has a preamble or title. In this case the preamble or title is postponed until the residue of the paper is gone through with.

Considering Proposition of Several Paragraphs

In considering a proposition consisting of several paragraphs, the course is for the whole paper to be read entirely through, in the first place, by the clerk; then a second time by the presiding officer, by paragraphs, pausing at the end of each, and putting questions for amending if amendments are proposed. When the whole paper has been gone through with in this manner, the presiding officer puts the final question on agreeing to or adopting the whole paper as amended or unamended.

Procedure on Order of Committee Reports

When a paper which has been referred to a committee and reported back to the assembly is taken up for consideration, the amendments only are first read by the clerk. The presiding officer then reads the first and puts it to the question, and so on until the whole

are adopted or rejected, before any other amendment
is admitted, with the exception of an amendment to an
amendment. When the amendments reported by the
committee have been thus disposed of, the presiding
officer pauses, and gives time for amendments to be
proposed in the assembly to the body of the paper
(which he also does if the paper has been reported
without amendments, putting no questions but on
amendments proposed) ; and when through the whole,
he puts the question on agreeing to or adopting the
paper, as the resolution, order, etc., of the assembly.

Stating of Final Question

The final question is sometimes stated merely on the
acceptance of the report, but a better form is on agreeing with the committee in the resolution, order, or
whatever else the conclusion of the report may be, as
amended, or without amendment. The resolution or
order is then to be entered in the journal as the resolution, etc., of the assembly, and not as the report of the
committee accepted.

Treatment of Amended Report

When the paper referred to a committee is reported
back, as amended, in a new draft (which may be and
often is done, where the amendments are numerous
and comparatively unimportant), the new draft is to
be considered as an amendment, and is to be first
amended, if necessary, and then put to the question as
an amendment reported by the committee. An alternative may be, first to accept the new draft, as a substitute for the original paper, and then to treat it as such.

Procedure When Several Questions Are Pending at the Same Time

It often happens that, besides a principal question,
there are several others connected with it, pending at
the same time, which are to be taken in their order;
as, for example, suppose, *first,* a principal motion;
second, a motion to amend; *third,* a motion to commit;

fourth, the preceding motions being pending, a question of order arises in the debate, which gives occasion, *fifth,* to a question of privilege, and this leads, *sixth,* to a subsidiary motion, as, to lie on the table. The regular course of proceeding requires the motion to lie on the table to be first put. If this is negatived, the question of privilege is then settled. After that comes the question of order; then the question of commitment; if that is negatived, the question of amendment is taken; and lastly the main question. This example will sufficiently illustrate the manner in which questions may grow out of one another and in what order they are to be decided.*

Stating of Question Before Action Is Taken

When a motion is made and seconded, it is the duty of the presiding officer to propose it to the assembly. Until this is done it is not a question before the assembly to be acted upon or considered in any manner, and consequently it is not then in order for any member to rise either to debate it or to make any motion in relation to it whatever. Should the presiding officer of an assembly refuse to put motions, or should he leave the assembly, transaction of business may continue, as in that case the vice-president is authorized to put any motion made according to rules and regulations.

Unparliamentary to State Principal and Subsidiary Motions Together

It is therefore a most unparliamentary and abusive proceeding to allow a principal motion and a subsidiary one relating to it to be proposed and stated together, and to be put to the question in their order, as is done when a member moves a principal question, a resolution, for example, and, at the same time, the previous question, or that the resolution lie on the table. In such a case the presiding officer should take no notice whatever of the subsidiary motion, but should propose the

* The order of motions, for the proposal of any question, is usually fixed by a special rule in legislative assemblies.

principal one by itself in the usual manner, before allowing any other to be made. Other members, then, would not be deprived of their rights of debate, etc., in relation to the subject moved.

Member Obtaining Floor Cannot Be Cut Off

When a member has obtained the floor he cannot be cut off from addressing the assembly on the question before it. At the same time, when speaking, he cannot be interrupted in his speech by any other member rising and moving an adjournment, or for the orders of the day, or by making any other privileged motion of the same kind; it being a general rule that a member in possession of the floor, or proceeding with his speech, cannot be taken down or interrupted, but by a call to order; and the question of order being decided, he is still to be heard through. A call for an adjournment, or for the orders of the day, or for the question, by gentlemen in their seats, is not a motion; as no motion can be made without rising and addressing the chair, and being called to by the presiding officer. Such calls for the question are themselves breaches of order.

CHAPTER XII

Order of Debate

The Distinction Between Debate in Deliberative Assembly and Forensic Debate

Debate in a deliberative assembly must be distinguished from forensic debate, or that which takes place before a judicial tribunal; the former being, in theory at least, more the expression of individual opinions among the members of the same body; the latter more a contest for victory, between the disputants, before a distinct and independent body; the former not admitting of replies, the latter regarding reply as the right of one of the parties.*

Presiding Officer Does Not Participate in Debate

It is a general rule, in all deliberative assemblies, that the presiding officer shall not participate in the debate, or other proceedings, in any other capacity than as such officer. He is only allowed, therefore, to state matters of fact within his knowledge; to inform the assembly on points of order or the course of proceeding, when called upon for that purpose, or when he finds it necessary to do so; and on appeals from his decision on questions of order; to address the assembly in debate.

* An exception to this rule is sometimes made in favor of the mover to a question, who is allowed, at the close of the debate, to reply to the arguments brought against his motion; but this is a matter of favor and indulgence, and not of right.

As to Manner of Speaking

Recognizing a Member
Desiring to Address the Assembly

When a member desires to address the assembly, on any subject before it (as well as to make a motion), he is to rise and stand up in his place, and to address himself not to the assembly, or any particular member, but to the presiding officer, who, on hearing him, calls to him by his name, that the assembly may take notice who it is that speaks, and give their attention accordingly. If any question arises as to who shall be entitled to the floor where several members rise at or nearly the same time, it is decided in the manner already described as to obtaining the floor to make a motion. (Page 46)

Preference Shown in Recognizing a Member

It is customary, indeed, for the presiding officer, after a motion has been made, seconded, and proposed, to give the floor to the mover,* in preference to others, if he rises to speak; or, on resuming a debate after an adjournment, to give the floor, if he desires it, to the mover of the adjournment in preference to other members; or, where two or more members claim the floor, to prefer him who is opposed to the measure in question; but in all these cases the determination of the presiding officer may be overruled by the assembly.

A Member Giving Up the Floor Loses It

It is sometimes thought that when a member, in the course of debate, breaks off his speech and gives up

---

* Sometimes a member, instead of proposing his motion at first, proceeds with his speech; but in such a case he is liable to be taken down to order, unless he states that he intends to conclude with a motion and informs the assembly what that motion is, and then he may be allowed to proceed.

the floor to another for a particular purpose, he is
entitled to it again, as of right, when that purpose is
accomplished; but, though this is generally conceded,
yet, when a member gives up the floor for one purpose,
he does so for all; and it is not possible for the presiding officer to take notice of and enforce agreements
of this nature between members.

Member Must Not Be Mentioned by Name in Debate

No person, in speaking, is to mention a member then
present by his name; but to describe him by his seat
in the assembly, or as the member who spoke last, or
last but one, or on the other side of the question, or
by some other equivalent expression. The purpose of
this rule is to guard as much as possible against the
excitement of all personal feeling, either of favor, or
of hostility, by separating, as it were, the official from
the personal character of each member, and having
regard to the former only in debate.

Presiding Officer's Prior Right to Speak

If the presiding officer rises to speak, any other
member who may have risen for the same purpose
ought to sit down, in order that the former may be first
heard; but this rule does not authorize the presiding
officer to interrupt a member while speaking, or to
cut off one to whom he has given the floor; he must
wait, like other members, until such member has done
speaking.

Position of Member While Speaking

A member while speaking must remain standing in
his place, and when he has finished his speech he ought
to resume his seat. But if he is unable to stand without
pain or inconvenience, in consequence of age, sickness,
or other infirmity, he may be indulged to speak sitting.

As to the Matter in Speaking

Debate Must Be Confined to the Question

Every question that can be made in a deliberative assembly is susceptible of being debated,* according to its nature; that is, every member has the right of expressing his opinion upon it. Hence it is a general rule, and the principal one relating to this matter, that in debate those who speak are to confine themselves to the question, and not to speak impertinently or beside the subject. So long as a member has the floor, and keeps within the rule, he may speak for as long a time as he pleases. Although, if an uninteresting speaker trespasses too much upon the time and patience of the assembly, the members seldom fail to show their dissatisfaction in some way or other, which induces him to bring his remarks to a close.

Indecent Language Proscribed

It is also a rule that no person, in speaking, is to use indecent language against the proceedings of the assembly, or to reflect upon any of its prior determinations, unless he means to conclude his remarks with a motion to rescind such determination; but while a proposition under consideration is still pending, and not adopted, though it may have been reported by a committee, reflections on it are no reflections on the assembly. The rule applies equally to the proceedings of committees, which are, indeed, the proceedings of the assembly.

Digression from Subject of Question Proscribed

Another rule in speaking is that no member is at liberty to digress from the matter of the question, to

* In legislative bodies it is usual to provide that certain questions, as, for example, to adjourn, to lie on the table, for the previous question, or, as to the order of business, shall be decided without debate.

fall upon the person of another, and to speak reviling, nipping, or unmannerly words of or to him. The nature of consequences of a measure may be reprobated in strong terms, but to arraign the motives of those who advocate it is a personality and against order.

When in Doubt as to Relevancy of Member's Remarks to Question

It is very often an extremely difficult and delicate matter to decide whether the remarks of a member are pertinent or relevant to the question; but it will, in general, be safe for the presiding officer to consider them so, unless they very clearly reflect, in an improper manner, either upon the person or motives of a member, or upon the proceedings of the assembly; or the member speaking digresses from or manifestly mistakes the question.

Particular Question Supersedes Main Question

It often happens in the consideration of a subject that, while the general question remains the same, the particular question before the assembly is constantly changing. Therefore, while, for example, the general question is on the adoption of a series of resolutions, the particular question may, at one moment be on an amendment; at another, on postponement; and, again, on the previous question. In all these cases, the particular question supersedes, for the time, the main question; and those who speak to it must confine their remarks accordingly. The enforcement of order, in this respect, requires the closest attention on the part of the presiding officer.

Procedure of Member After Being Called to Order

When a member is interrupted by the presiding officer, or called to order by a member, for irrelevancy or departing from the question, a question may be made as to whether he shall be allowed to proceed in his remarks, in the manner he was speaking when he was interrupted; but if no question is made, or if one is made and decided in the negative, he is still to be allowed to proceed in order, that is abandoning the objectionable course of remarks.

As to Times of Speaking

No Member Shall Speak More Than Once

The general rule in all deliberative assemblies, unless it is otherwise specially provided, is that no member shall speak more than once to the same question, although the debate on that question may be adjourned and continued through several days, and although a member who desires to speak a second time has, in the course of the debate, changed his opinion.*

Relevant to General Rule Next Above Cited

This rule refers to the same question, technically considered; for if a resolution is moved and debated, and then referred to a committee, those who speak on the introduction of the motion may speak again on the question presented by the report of the committee, though it is substantially the same question with the former. And so, members who have spoken on the principal or main question may speak again on all the subsidiary or incidental questions arising in the course of the debate.

Provision by Which a Member May Speak a Second Time

The rule, as to speaking but once on a question, if strictly enforced, will prevent a member from speaking

---

* This is a rule in the United States House of Representatives restraining a member from speaking more than once to the same question without leave of the House, unless the member is the mover, proposer, or introducer of the matter pending, under which circumstances he is allowed to speak in reply; but only when every other member who desires to speak has spoken.

a second time without the general consent of the assembly, so long as there is any other member who himself desires to speak. On the other hand, when all who desire to speak have spoken, a member may speak a second time by leave of the assembly.

May Speak a Second Time to Make Explanation

A member may also be permitted to speak a second time, in the same debate, in order to clear a matter of fact; or merely to explain himself in some material part of his speech; or to the orders of the assembly, if they be transgressed (although no question may be made), but carefully keeping within that line and not falling into the matter itself.

Cannot Interrupt Another Member to Explain

It is sometimes supposed that, because a member has a right to explain himself he therefore has a right to interrupt another member while speaking, in order to make the explanation; but this is a mistake. He should wait until the member speaking has finished; and if a member, on being requested, yields the floor for an explanation, he relinquishes it altogether.

As to Stopping Debate

Ending Debate by Ordering the Previous Question

The only mode in use in this country, until recently, for the purpose of putting an end to an unprofitable or tiresome debate, was by moving the previous question. The effect of this motion, as already explained, if decided in the affirmative, is to require the main or principal question to be immediately taken. When this question is moved, therefore, it necessarily suspends all further consideration of the main question, and precludes all further debate or amendment of it;

though, as has been seen, it stands in the same degree with postponement, amendment, and commitment.

Fixing of Time to End Debate

The other mode of putting an end to debate, which has recently been introduced into use, is for the assembly to adopt beforehand a special order in reference to a particular subject, that, at such a time specified, all debate upon it shall cease, and all motions or questions pending in relation to it shall be decided.

Shortening Debate by Limiting Time

Another rule, which has been introduced for the purpose of shortening rather than stopping debate, is, that no member shall be permitted to speak more than a certain specified time on any question; so that, when the time allotted has expired, the presiding officer announces the fact, and the member speaking resumes his seat.

Some time ago a rule was adopted, by the British House of Commons (termed "closure," also "clôture"), that debate may be closed at any time by a *majority vote,* if the discussion leads to disorder in the House or hinders its business. When debate is so closed the question may be immediately decided by the House. The United States Congress has adopted this rule.

In several foreign parliaments the "clôture" is proposed when occasion requires. In the Belgian lower house the prime minister and president of the chamber confer as to the advisability of "clôture."

In Denmark when a debate is prolonged beyond proper limits, the president may propose the "clôture," and the decision is made by the chamber without debate. The president of the house, in Spain, may move the "clôture."

As to Decorum in Debate

Disturbing of Member While Speaking Proscribed

Every member having the right to be heard, every other member is bound to conduct himself in such a manner that this right may be effectual. Hence it is a rule of order, as well as of decency, that no member is to disturb another in his speech by hissing, coughing, spitting; by speaking or whispering; by passing between the presiding officer and the member speaking; by going across the assemby-room, or walking up and down in it; or by any other disorderly deportment which tends to disturb or disconcert a member who is speaking.

When Disrespect to a Speaking Member Is Evident He Should Sit Down

But, if a member speaking finds that he is not regarded with that respectful attention which his equal right demands—that it is not the inclination of the assembly to hear him—and that by conversation or any other noise they endeavor to drown his voice—it is his most prudent course to submit himself to the pleasure of the assembly, and to sit down; for it scarcely ever happens that the members of an assembly are guilty of this piece of ill manners without some excuse or provocation, or that they are so wholly inattentive to one who says anything worth their hearing.

To Maintain Order Is Duty of Presiding Officer

It is the duty of the presiding officer, in such a case, to endeavor to reduce the assembly to order and decorum; but, if his repeated calls to order, and his appeals to the good sense and decency of the members, prove ineffectual, it then becomes his duty to call by name any member who obstinately persists in irregularity; whereupon the assembly may require such member to withdraw, who is then to be heard, if he desires it, in exculpation, and to withdraw. Then the presiding officer states the offense committed, and the assembly takes under consideration the kind and degree of punishment to be inflicted.

When Disorder May Be Permitted

If, on repeated trials, the presiding officer finds that the assembly will not support him in the exercise of his authority, he will then be justified, but not till then, in permitting, without censure, every kind of disorder.

As to Disorderly Words

Offensive Language

If a member, in speaking, makes use of language which is personally offensive to another, or insulting to the assembly, and the member offended, or any other, thinks proper to complain of it to the assembly, the course of proceeding is as follows:

Treatment of Offending Member

The member speaking is immediately interrupted in the course of his speech by another or several members rising and calling to order, and the member who objects or complains of the words, is then called upon by the presiding officer to state the words which he complains of, repeating them exactly as he conceives them to have been spoken, in order that they may be reduced to writing by the clerk; or the member complaining, without being so called upon, may proceed at once to state the words either verbally or in writing, and desire that the clerk may take them down at the table. The presiding officer may then direct the clerk to take them down; but if he sees the objection to be a trivial one and thinks there is no foundation for their being thought disorderly, he will prudently

delay giving any such directions, in order not un-
necessarily to interrupt the proceedings. Although if
the members generally seem to be in favor of having
the words taken down, by calling out to that effect,
or by a vote, which the assembly may doubtless pass,
the presiding officer should certainly order the clerk
to take them down, in the form and manner in which
they are stated by the member who objects.

Denial by Member of Offensive Language

The words objected to being thus written down and
forming a part of the minutes in the clerk's book,
they are next to be read to the member who was
speaking, who may deny that those are the words
which he spoke, in which case the assembly must decide by a question whether they are the words or
not.* If he does not deny that he spoke those words,
or when the assembly has itself determined what the
words are, then the member may either justify them
or explain the sense in which he used them, so as to
remove the objection of their being disorderly; or he
may make an apology for them.

No Further Proceeding When
Explanation or Apology Is Accepted

If the justification, or explanation, or apology of
the member is thought sufficient by the assembly, no
further proceeding is necessary. The member may resume and go on with his speech, the assembly being
presumed, unless some further motion is made, to be
satisfied. However, if any two members (one to make
and the other to second the motion) think it necessary
to state a question, so as to take the sense of the assembly upon the words and whether the member in
using them has been guilty of any offense towards the
assembly, the member must withdraw before that question is stated; and then the sense of the assembly must

* The words, as written down, may be amended, so as to conform
to what the assembly thinks to be the truth.

be taken, and such further proceedings had in relation to punishing the member as may be thought necessary and proper.

Writing Down Offensive Language

The above is the course of proceeding established by the writers of greatest authority,* and ought invariably to be pursued. It might, however, be improved, by the member who objects to words, writing them down at once, and thereupon moving that they be made a part of the minutes; by which means the presiding officer would be relieved from the responsibility of determining, in the first instance, upon the character of the words.

Prompt Notice Should Be Taken of Offensive Words

If offensive words are not taken notice of at the time they are spoken, but the member is allowed to finish his speech,† and then any other person speaks, or any other matter of business intervenes before notice is taken of the words which gave offense, the words are not to be written down, or the member using them censured. This rule is established for the common security of all the members, and to prevent the mistakes which must necessarily happen if words complained of are not immediately reduced to writing.

* Mr. Hatsell, in England, and Mr. Jefferson, in this country.

† Mr. Jefferson lays it down, that "disorderly words are not to be noticed till the member has finished his speech." But in this he is contradicted by Hatsell, as well as by the general practice of legislative bodies.

CHAPTER XIII

Of the Question

Distinction Between Question, Motion, etc.

When any proposition is made to a deliberative assembly, it is called a *motion;* when it is stated or propounded to the assembly for their acceptance or rejection, it is termed a *question;* and when adopted, it becomes the *order, resolution,* or *vote* of the assembly.

Object of All Foregoing Proceedings

All the proceedings which have thus far been considered have only had for their object to bring a proposition into a form to be put to the question; that is, to be adopted as the sense, will or judgment of the assembly, or to be rejected; according as such proposition may be found to unite in its favor, or to fail of uniting, a majority of the members.

Final Vote

When any proposition, whether principal, subsidiary, or incidental, or of whatever nature it may be, is made, seconded, and stated, if no alteration is proposed—or if it admits of none, or if it is amended—and the debate upon it, if any, appears to be brought to a close, the presiding officer then inquires, whether the assembly is ready for the question, and, if no person rises, the question is then stated, and the votes of the assembly taken upon it.

The several ways of voting are: (*a*) By silent assent; (*b*) by voice; (*c*) by holding up hands; (*d*) by division; (*e*) by roll call; (*f*) by ballot; (*g*) by yeas and nays.

Question to Be Stated in Form It Will Appear on Journal

The question is not always stated to the assembly in the precise form in which it arises or is introduced; thus, for example, when a member presents a petition, or the chairman of a commitee offers a report, the question which arises, if no motion is made is, *Shall the petition or the report be received?* and so, when the previous question is moved, it is stated in this form, *Shall the main question be now put?*—the question being stated, in all cases, in the form in which it will appear on the journal, if it passes in the affirmative.

Consent of Assembly Taken for Granted in Unimportant Matters

In matters of trifling importance, or which are generally of course, such as receiving petitions and reports, withdrawing motions, reading papers, etc., the presiding officer most commonly supposes or takes for granted the consent of the assembly, where no objection is expressed, and does not go through the formality of taking the question by a vote. But if, after a vote has been taken in this informal way and declared, any member rises to object, the presiding officer should consider everything that has passed as nothing, and at once go back and pursue the regular course of proceeding. Thus, if a petition is received without a question, and the clerk is proceeding to read it, in the usual order of business, if any one rises to object, it will be the safest and most proper course for the presiding officer to require a motion for receiving it to be regularly made and seconded.

Putting Final Question

The question being stated by the presiding officer, he first puts it in the affirmative, namely: *As many as are of opinion that*—repeating the words of the question—*say aye;* and, immediately, all the members who are of that opinion answer *aye;* the presiding officer then puts the question negatively: *As many as are of a different opinion, say no;* and, thereupon, all the members who are of that opinion answer *no.* The presiding officer judges by his ear which side has "the mores voices," and decides accordingly, that *the ayes have it,* or *the noes have it,* as the case may be. If the presiding officer is doubtful as to the majority of voices, he may put the question a second time, and if he is still unable to decide, or, if, having decided according to his judgment, any member arises and declares that he believes the *ayes* or the *noes* (whichever it may be) *have it,* contrary to the declaration of the presiding officer,* then the presiding officer directs the assembly to divide, in order that the members on the one side and the other may be counted.

When Too Late to Divide Assembly

If, however, any new motion should be made, after the presiding officer's declaration, or, if a member who was not in the assembly room when the question was taken, should come in, it will then be too late to contradict the presiding officer, and have the assembly divided.

Manner of Voting

The above is the parliamentary form of taking a question, and is in general use in this country; but in some of our legislative assemblies, and especially in those of the New England States, the suffrages are given by the members holding up their right hands, first those in the affirmative, and then those in the negative, of the question. If the presiding officer cannot determine by the show of hands which side has the majority, he may call upon the members to vote again, and if he is still in doubt, or if his declaration is questioned, a division takes place. When the question is taken in this manner, the presiding officer di-

* The most common expression is: "I doubt the vote," or, "that vote is doubted."

rects the members, first on the affirmative side and then on the negative, to manifest their opinion by holding up the right hand.

Counting the Divided Assembly

When a division of the assembly takes place, the presiding officer sometimes directs the members to range themselves on different sides of the assembly room, and either counts them himself or they are counted by tellers appointed by him for the purpose, or by monitors permanently appointed for that and other purposes; or the members rise in their seats, first on the affirmative and then on the negative, and are counted in the same manner. When the members are counted by the presiding officer, he announces the numbers and declares the result. When they are counted by tellers or monitors, the tellers must first agree among themselves, and then the one who has told for the majority reports the numbers to the presiding officer, and the presiding officer declares the result.

Counting the Divided Assembly by Tellers

The best mode of dividing an assembly that is at all numerous, is for the presiding officer to appoint tellers for each division or section of the assembly room, and then to require the members, first those in the affirmative, and then those in the negative, to rise and be counted. When this has been done, on each side, the tellers of the several divisions make their returns, and the presiding officer declares the result.

In Equal Division of Assembly, Presiding Officer Must Vote

Formerly, when members were unequally divided, the presiding officer could give, or refrain from giving, the casting vote, as he chose, and should he refrain from voting the motion would not prevail and the decision would be in the negative, but now the law requires the speaker in the United States House of Representa-

tives to cast his vote when it would be the deciding
vote. The occasions upon which this rule applies, according to the practice in the House are: (*a*) When
necessary to break a tie; (*b*) to make a tie; (*c*) to complete a two-thirds vote; (*d*) to make a quorum. However, on an even division, the rule has been interpreted
by some as not including an even division; but this
interpretation does not now obtain in Congress, nor
in public assemblies in general, where the rule is now
established that the speaker must vote on an equal
division, notwithstanding that he may vote in the negative. But the right of the speaker to vote is in some
cases subject to positive law, as, for instance, where
he is not a member of the body over which he presides
he has no right to vote, unless so provided by the law,
or is prescribed by the Constitution, as referred to
the Vice-President of the United States, who has the
right to give a casting vote. This applies also to the
lieutenant-governors of some states, who vote by the
virtue of a constitutional provision, whereas, otherwise, not being members of the bodies over which they
preside, they would have no right to vote. But no rule
of any organized body, of which the speaker is a member, can prevent him legally from exercising his right
to vote, which is not in any sense forfeited by the
fact of his having been elected speaker. Furthermore,
the speaker is not required to vote in regular order,
as are other members under the rule; but may claim
and exercise his right to vote afterwards should he
have failed to vote in regular order.

Every Member Bound to Vote

It is a general rule that every member who is in
the assembly room at the time when the question is
stated has not only the right but is bound to vote;
and, on the other hand, that no member can vote who
was not in the room at that time.

Silence, on the part of the majority in an assembly,
when a question is put by the presiding officer, is taken
as assent, unless the question has reference to some
revolutionary measure foreign to the process established to ascertain the general will, and to which the

members have not assented to beforehand with full
knowledge of its nature and import.

When a whole assembly is silent, by which a unanimous vote in the affirmative is implied, and there are
some present who have the right and opportunity to
vote and do not exercise it, and offer no objection to
the passage of any act by the regular manner of voting,
etc., no objection can afterwards be made upon the
grounds of an insufficient or invalid vote.

Taking the Question by Yeas and Nays

The only other form of taking the question which
requires to be described is one in general use in this
country, by means of which the names of the members voting on the one side and on the other are ascertained and entered in the journal of the assembly.
This mode, which is peculiar to the legislative bodies
of the United States, is called taking the question
by yeas and nays. In order to take a question in this
manner it is stated on both sides at once, namely: *As
many as are of opinion that, etc., will, when their
names are called, answer Yes; and, As many as are of
a different opinion will, when their names are called,
answer No;* the roll of the assembly is then called
over by the clerk, and each member, as his name is
called, rises in his place, and answers *yes* or *no*, and
the clerk notes the answer as the roll is called. When
the roll has been gone through the clerk reads over
first the names of those who have answered in the
affirmative and then the names of those who have
answered in the negative in order that if he has made
any mistake in noting the answer, or if any member has made a mistake in his answer, the mistake
of either may be corrected. The names having been
thus read over, and the mistakes, if any, corrected,
the clerk counts the numbers on each side, and reports
them to the presiding officer, who declares the result
to the assembly.

In both Houses of the United States Congress the
Constitution requires that the yeas and nays of the
members, on any question, if desired by one-fifth of

those present, shall be entered on the journal; and the entry must be made without any order in voting for or against a vetoed bill.

Taking a Question by Yeas and Nays in Massachusetts

The following is the mode practiced in the House of Representatives of Massachusetts (which was once one of the most numerous of all the legislative bodies in this country) of taking a question by yeas and nays. The names of the members being printed on a sheet, the clerk calls them in their order; and as each one answers, the clerk (responding to the member, at the same time) places a figure in pencil, expressing the number of the answer, at the left or right of the name, according as the answer is yes or no; so that the last figure or number, on each side, shows the number of the answers on that side; and the last two numbers or figures represent the respective numbers of the affirmatives and negatives on the division. Thus, at the left hand of the name of the member who first answers *yes,* the clerk places a figure 1; at the right hand of the first member who answers *no,* he also places a figure 1; the second member that answers *yes* is marked 2; and so on to the end of the list; the side of the name, on which the figure is placed, denoting whether the answer is *yes* or *no,* and the figure denoting the number of the answer on that side. The affirmatives and negatives are then read separately, if necessary, though this is usually omitted, and the clerk is then prepared, by means of the last figure on each side, to give the numbers to the speaker to be announced to the house. The names and answers are afterwards recorded on the journal.

Question Cannot Be Opened and Debate Renewed When Vote by Yeas and Nays Has Begun

In any of the modes of taking a question, in which it is first put on one side, and then on the other, it is no full question until the negative as well as the affirmative has been put. Consequently, until the negative has been put it is in order for any member, in the same manner as if the division had not commenced, to rise and speak, make motions for amendment or otherwise, and thus renew the debate; and this whether such member was in the assembly room or not when the question was put and partly taken. In such a case the question must be put over again on the affirmative as well as the negative side, for the reason that members who were not in the assembly room when the question was first put may have since come in, and also that some of those who voted may have changed their minds. When a question is taken by yeas and nays, and the negative as well as the affirmative of the question is stated, and the voting on each side begins and proceeds at the same time, the question cannot be opened and the debate renewed after the voting has commenced. But, unless it be a ballot, a member may change his vote at any time prior to the announced result. In the United States Senate, however, a member may change or withdraw his vote by unanimous consent.

Questions Arising During a Division

If any question arises in a point of order, for example, as to the right or the duty of a member to vote during a division, the presiding officer must decide it peremptorily, subject to the revision and correction of the assembly, after the division is over. In a case of this kind there can be no debate, though the presiding officer may if he pleases receive the assistance of members with their advice, which they are to give sitting, in order to avoid even the appearance of a debate; but this can only be with the leave of the presiding officer, as otherwise the division might be prolonged to an inconvenient length. Nor can any question be taken, for otherwise there might be division upon division without end.

No Decision upon a Count
Unless a Quorum Is Present

When, from counting the assembly on a division, it appears that there is not a quorum present, there is no decision; but the matter in question continues in the same state in which it was before the division; and, when afterwards resumed, whether on the same or some future day, it must be taken up at that precise point.

CHAPTER XIV

Of Reconsideration

When a Decision Is Final

It is a principle of parliamentary law upon which many of the rules and proceedings are founded, that when a question has been put once to a deliberative assembly, and decided, whether in the affirmative or negative, that decision is the judgment of the assembly, and cannot be again brought into question.

Principle Next Above Stated Applies to Equivalent Questions

This principle holds equally although the question proposed is not the identical question which has already been decided, but only its equivalent; as, for example, where the negative of one question amounts to the affirmative of the other, and leaves no other alternative, these questions are the equivalents of one another, and a decision of the one necessarily concludes the other.

Explanation of Rule Next Above

A common application of the rule as to equivalent questions occurs in the case of an amendment proposed by striking out words, in which it is the invariable practice to consider the negative of striking out as equivalent to the affirmative of agreeing; so that to put a question on agreeing, after a question on striking out is negatived, would be, in effect, to put the same question twice over.

When a Question May Be Proposed Again

The principle above stated does not apply so as to prevent putting the same question in the different stages of any proceeding, as, for example, in legislative bodies, the different stages of a bill. Therefore, in considering reports of committees, questions already taken and decided, before the subject was referred, may be again proposed; and, in like manner, orders of the assembly, and instructions or references to committees, may be discharged or rescinded.

Reconsideration Allowed for Sufficient Reason

The inconvenience of this rule, which is still maintained in all its strictness in the British Parliament (though various expedients are there resorted to, to counteract or evade it), has led to the introduction into the parliamentary practice of this country of the motion for *reconsideration*. While this recognizes and upholds the rule in all its ancient strictness, it allows a deliberative assembly, for sufficient reasons, to relieve itself from the embarrassment and inconvenience which would occasionally result from a strict enforcement of the rule in a particular case.

Common Practice to Reconsider Vote Already Passed

It has now come to be a common practice in all our deliberative assemblies, and may consequently be considered as a principle of the common parliamentary law of this country, to reconsider a vote already passed, whether affirmatively or negatively, and the final result only is operative.

Reconsideration by Assembly of a Vote Rejecting Amendment

For this purpose a motion is made and seconded, in the usual manner, that such a vote be reconsidered; and if this motion prevails, the matter stands before the assembly in precisely the same state and condition, and the same questions are to be put in relation to it as if the vote reconsidered had never been passed. Thus, if an amendment by inserting words is moved and rejected, the same amendment cannot be moved again; but the assembly may reconsider the vote by which it was rejected, and then the question will recur on the amendment, precisely as if the former vote had never been passed.

Special Rule to Regulate Making of Motion to Reconsider

It is usual in legislative bodies to regulate by a special rule the time, manner, and by whom a motion to reconsider may be made; thus, for example, that it shall be made only on the same or a succeeding day—by a member who voted with the majority—or at a time when there are as many members present as there were when the vote was passed; but, where there is no special rule on the subject, a motion to reconsider must be considered in the same light as any other motion, and as subject to no other rules.

Such a motion cannot be withdrawn after the "succeeding day" without consent of the body is the rule in the United States House of Representatives; but in the Senate the rule is, that, if a motion to reconsider is lost, or if carried, and the first decision of the reconsidered question is affirmed, a motion to reconsider cannot be renewed without unanimous consent.

CHAPTER XV

Committees, Their Nature and Functions

Formation

It is usual in all deliberative assemblies to take the preliminary (sometimes, also, the intermediate) measures, and to prepare matters to be acted upon, in the assembly by means of committees, composed either of members specially selected for the particular occasion, or appointed beforehand for all matters of the same nature.

How Termed

Committees of the first kind are usually called *select*, the others *standing;* though the former appellation belongs with equal propriety to both, in order to distinguish them from another form of committee, constituted either for a particular occasion, or for all cases of a certain kind, which is composed of all the members of the assembly, and therefore denominated a *committee of the whole*.

Advantages

The advantages of proceeding in this mode are manifold. It enables a deliberative assembly to do many things, which, from its members, it would otherwise be unable to do—to accomplish a much greater quantity of business, by dividing it among the members, than could possibly be accomplished, if the whole body were obliged to devote itself to each particular subject —and to act in the preliminary and preparatory steps, with a greater degree of freedom, than is compatible with the forms of proceeding usually observed in full assembly.

Purpose of Appointment

Committees are appointed to consider a particular subject, either at large or under special instructions: to obtain information in reference to a matter before the assembly, either by personal inquiry and inspection, or by the examination of witnesses; and to digest and put into the proper form, for the adoption of the assembly, all resolutions, votes, orders, and other papers with which they may be charged. Committees are commonly said to be the "eyes and ears" of the assembly; it is equally true that, for certain purposes, they are also its "head and hands."

Powers and Functions

The powers and functions of committees depend chiefly upon the authority and particular instructions given them by the assembly at the time of their appointment. But they may also be, and very often are, further instructed while they are in the exercise of their functions. Sometimes it even happens that these additional instructions wholly change the nature of a committee by charging it with inquiries quite different from those for which it was originally established.

Standing and Select Committees, Same Manner of Appointing

In the manner of appointing committees there is no difference between standing and other select committees as to the mode of selecting the members to compose them; and in reference to committees of the whole, as there is no selection of members, they are appointed simply by the order of the assembly.

Number Appointed

In the appointment of select committees, the first thing to be done is to fix upon the number. This is usually effected in the same manner that blanks are filled, namely, by members proposing, without the formality of a motion, such numbers as they please, which are then separately put to the question, beginning with the largest and going regularly through to the smallest, until the assembly comes to a vote.

Selection of Committees

The number being settled, there are three modes of selecting the members, as follows: By appointment of the presiding officer—by ballot—and by nomination and vote of the assembly. The first is sometimes in virtue of a standing rule, sometimes in pursuance of a vote of the assembly in a particular case. The second is always in pursuance of a vote. The last is the usual course when no vote is taken.

Usually Presiding Officer Names Committee

In deliberative assemblies, whose sittings are of considerable length, as legislative bodies, it is usual to provide by a standing rule that, unless otherwise ordered in a particular case, all committees shall be named by the presiding officer. Where this is the case, whenever a committee is ordered, and the number settled, the presiding officer at once names the members to compose it. Sometimes, also, the rule fixes the number of which, unless otherwise ordered, committees shall consist. This mode of appointing a committee is frequently resorted to where there is no rule on the subject.

Appointing by Ballot

When a committee is ordered to be appointed by ballot, the members are chosen by the assembly, either singly or all together, as may be ordered, in the same manner that other elections are made; and, in such elections, as in other cases of the election of the officers of the assembly, a majority of all the votes given in is necessary to a choice.

Appointing by Nomination and Vote

When a committee is directed to be appointed by nomination and vote, the names of the members proposed are put to the question singly, and approved or rejected by the assembly, by a vote taken in the usual manner. If the nomination is directed to be made by the presiding officer, he may propose the names in the same manner, or all at once; the former mode being the most direct and simple; the latter enabling the assembly to vote more understandingly upon the several names proposed. When the nomination is directed to be made at large, the presiding officer calls upon the assembly to nominate, and names being mentioned accordingly, he puts to vote the first name he hears.

Reviving Committee

It is also a compendious mode of appointing a committee, to revive one which has already discharged itself by a report; or by charging a committee appointed for one purpose with some additional duty, of the same or a different character.

Referring of a Bill to Unbiased Committee

In regard to the appointment of committees, so far as the selection of the members is concerned, it is a general rule in legislative bodies, when a bill is to be referred, that none who speak directly against the body of it are to be of the committee, for the reason that he who would totally destroy will not amend; but that, for the opposite reason, those who only take exception to some particulars in the bill are to be of the committee. This rule supposes the purpose of the commitment to be not the consideration of the general merits of the bill, but the amendment of it in its particular provisions, so as to make it acceptable to the assembly.

Majority Should Be Favorable to Subject

This rule, of course, is only for the guidance of the presiding officer and the members, in the exercise of their discretion; as the assembly may refuse from serving, or may itself appoint on a committee persons who are opposed to the subject referred. It is customary, however, in all deliberative assemblies to constitute a committee of such persons (the mover and seconder of a measure being of course appointed), a majority of whom, at least, are favorably inclined to the measure proposed.

Notifying Committee of Appointment

When a committee has been appointed in reference to a particular object, it is the duty of the secretary of the assembly to make out a list of the members, together with a certified copy of the authority or instructions under which they are to act, and to give the papers to the member first named on the list of the committee, if convenient, but, otherwise, to any other member of the committee.

Organization and Manner of Procedure

The Chairman

The person first named on a committee acts as its chairman, or presiding officer, so far as relates to the preliminary steps to be taken, and is usually permitted to do so through the whole proceedings; but this is a matter of courtesy, every committee having a right to elect its own chairman, who presides over it, and makes the report of its proceedings to the assembly.

Time and Place of Meeting

A committee is properly to receive directions from the assembly, as to the time and place of its meeting, and cannot regularly sit at any other time and place. It may be ordered to sit immediately, while the assembly is sitting, and make its report forthwith.

When Committee Is Not Permitted to Sit

When no directions are given, a committee may select its own time and place of meeting; but, without a special order to that effect, it is not at liberty to sit while the assembly sits; and, if a committee is sitting, when the assembly comes to order after an adjournment, it is the duty of the chairman to rise, instantly, on being certified of it, and, with the other members, to attend the service of the assembly.

Procedure

In regard to its forms of proceeding, a committee is essentially a miniature assembly—it can only act when regularly assembled together as a committee, and not by separate consultation and consent of the members; nothing being the agreement or report of a committee but what is agreed to in that manner—a vote taken in committee is as binding as a vote of the assembly—a majority of the members is necessary to constitute a quorum for business, unless a larger or smaller number has been fixed by the assembly itself—and a committee has full power over whatever may be committed to it, except that it is not at liberty to change the title or subject.

When a Committee Is Free to Meet Where It Pleases

A committee, which is under no directions as to the time and place of meeting, may meet when and where it pleases, and adjourn itself from day to day, or otherwise until it has gone through with the business committed to it. However, if it is ordered to meet at a particular time, and it fails to do so, for any cause, the committee is closed, and cannot act without being newly directed to sit.

Disorderly Words Spoken

Disorderly words spoken in a committee must be written down in the same manner as in the assembly; but the committee, as such, can do nothing more than report them to the assembly for its animadversion. Neither can a committee punish disorderly conduct of any other kind, but must report it to the assembly.

Order of Proceeding

When any paper is before a committee, whether select or of the whole, it may either have originated with the committee or have been referred to it. In either case when the paper comes to be considered, the course for it is to be first read entirely through by the clerk of the committee, if there is one, otherwise by the chairman. Then it should be read through again by paragraphs by the chairman, pausing at the end of each paragraph, and putting questions for amending, either by striking out or inserting, if proposed. This is the natural order of proceeding in considering and amending any paper, and is to be adhered to strictly in the assembly. However, the same strictness does not seem necessary in a committee.

Original Paper, How Treated

If the paper before a committee is one which has originated with the committee, questions are put on amendments proposed, but not on agreeing to the several paragraphs of which it is composed, separately, as they are gone through with; this being reserved for the close, when a question is to be put on the whole for agreeing to the paper as amended or unamended.

Referred Papers, How Treated

If the paper be one which has been referred to the committee, they proceed as in the other case to put questions of amendment, if proposed, but no final question on the whole. This is because all the parts of the paper having been passed upon, if not adopted by the assembly as the basis of its action, stand, of course, unless altered or struck out by a vote of the assembly. And even if the committee are opposed to the whole paper, and are of opinion that it cannot be made good by amendments, they have no authority to reject it. They must report it back to the assembly, without amendments (specially stating their objections, if they think proper), and there make their opposition as individual members.*

Report on Paper Originating with Committee

In the case of a paper originating with a committee, they may erase or interline it as much as they please; though, when finally agreed to, it ought to be reported in a clear draft, fairly written, without erasure or interlineation.

Report on Paper Referred to Committee

But, in the case of a paper referred to a committee, they are not at liberty to erase, interline, blot, disfigure, or tear it, in any manner. They must, in a separate paper, set down the amendments they have agreed to report, stating the words which are to be inserted or omitted, and the places where the amendments are to be made, by references to the paragraph or section, line, and word.

Amended Draft by Committee

If the amendments agreed to are very numerous and minute, the committee may report them altogether, in the form of a new and amended draft.

When Committee Has Agreed upon a Report

When a committee has gone through the paper, or agreed upon a report on the subject, which has been referred to them, it is then moved by some member, and thereupon voted, that the committee rise, and that the chairman, or some other member, make their report to the assembly.

Making Report to the Assembly

When the report of a committee is to be made, the chairman, or member appointed to make the report,

---

* This rule is not applicable, of course, to those cases in which the *subject* (as well as the *form* or *details* of a paper) is referred to the committee.

standing in his place, informs the assembly that the committee to whom was referred such a subject or paper have, according to order, had the same under consideration, and have directed him to make a report thereon, or to report the same with sundry amendments, or without amendment, as the case may be, which he is ready to do when the assembly shall please; and he or any other member may then move that the report be now received. On this motion being made, the question is put whether the assembly will receive the report at that time, and a vote passes, accordingly, either to receive it then, or fixing upon some future time for its reception.

Delivering Report

At the time when, by the order of the assembly, the report is to be received, the chairman reads it in his place, and then delivers it, together with all the papers connected with it, to the clerk at the table, where it is again read, and then lies on the table until the time assigned, or until it suits the convenience of the assembly to take it up for consideration.

A Report with Amendments

If the report of the committee is of a paper with amendments, the chairman reads the amendments with the coherence in the paper, whatever it may be, and opens the alterations, and the reasons of the committee for the amendments, until he has gone through the whole. When the report is read at the clerk's table, the amendments only are read without the coherence.

Reports Without Motions

In practice, however, the formality of a motion and vote on the reception of a report is usually dispensed with. Although, if any objection is made, or if the presiding officer sees any informality in the report, he should decline receiving it without a motion and vote. Moreover, a report, if of any considerable length, is seldom read, either by the chairman in his place or by the clerk at the table, until it is taken up for consideration. In legislative assemblies the printing of reports generally renders the reading of them unnecessary.

Dissolving of Committee

The report of a committee being made and received, the committee is dissolved, and can act no more without a new power; but their authority may be revived by a vote, and the same matter recommitted to them. If a report, when offered to the assembly, is not received, the committee is not thereby discharged, but may be ordered to sit again, and a time and place appointed accordingly.

Recommitting of Report

When a subject or paper has been once committed, and a report made upon it, it may be recommitted either to the same or a different committee. If a report is recommitted, before it has been agreed to by the assembly, what has heretofore passed in the committee is of no validity; the whole question being again before the committee as if nothing had passed there in relation to it.

Forms of Report

The report of a committee may be made in three different forms, namely: *first*, it may contain merely a statement of facts, reasoning, or opinion, in relation to the subject of it, without any specific conclusion; or, *second*, a statement of facts, reasoning, or opinion, concluding with a resolution, or series of resolutions, or some other specific proposition; or, *third*, it may consist merely of such resolutions, or propositions, without any introductory part.

Question on Receiving a Report

The first question on a report is, in strictness, on receiving it; though in practice this question is seldom or never made; the consent of the assembly, especially in respect to the report of a committee of the whole, being generally presumed unless objection is made. When a report is received, whether by general consent, or upon a question and vote, the committee is discharged, and the report becomes the basis of the future proceedings of the assembly on the subject to which it relates.

Adoption or Acceptance of Reports

The report of a committee having been presented to the assembly, and either read or given to the secretary or chair, there then follows in order the proper disposition of the report which depends upon the nature of the same.

(a) There is no necessity for action on a report, and the reporting member makes no motion for its disposal when the report relates only to an opinion or a statement of fact, and no motion is made by the reporting member for its disposal. The proper motion, however, to be made should any action be taken, is ''to accept'' the report, thereby fixing the responsibility for the statement upon the assembly, as the act of acceptance is equivalent to an endorsement.

A report relating to finance, as made by treasurers or boards of trustees, should be submitted to and verified by an auditing committee, as an assembly cannot when voting to accept the report guarantee the accuracy of the figures, and it is a function of the chair when a financial report is made to announce, without any motion, that it has been referred to the auditing committee. But should there not be an auditing committee, then a motion should be made to refer the report to an auditing committee to be appointed by the chair, and when the report is reported on by the auditing committee, it should then be accepted or adopted, which act becomes a complete endorsement of all that the report contains.

(b) Recommendations in a report not in the form of motions should all appear at the end of the report, and motion made to adopt the recommendations, even though they may have previously been given separately.

(c) Whenever practicable, where a report ends with one or a series of resolutions, the reporting member should move that the resolution or resolutions be adopted or agreed to.

(d) When a resolution is reported back by a committee to which it was referred, and the motion to postpone indefinitely is pending, it becames ignored; but an amendment, if pending, should be reported on. The recommendation of the committee determines the form of the question to be stated by the chairman, *e. g., First,* when the committee can come to no agreement and makes no recommendation, or when it does recommend its adoption, the question should be stated on the amendment, if one should be pending, and then on the resolution. These motions should not be repeated, as they were pending when the question was referred to the committee. *Second,* when the recommendation is against the adoption of the resolution, the form of stating the question on the resolution is as follows: "The question is on the adoption of the resolution, the recommendation of the committee to the contrary notwithstanding." Should it be recommended by the committee not to adopt an amendment a like course is taken. *Third,* when a resolution or paper with amendments is reported back by the committee, the amendments only should be read by the reporting member, and sufficiently in detail to render them clear to all present. He should then move their adoption, and after the chairman has stated the question on the adoption, he directs that the first amendment be read, which being done, leaves it open for debate and amendment. After the vote is taken on this amendment, the others are read in turn, until the amendments admitting amendments only to those of the committee, are adopted or rejected. After the committee's amendments have been disposed of, other amendments, if any, may be proposed, and after being voted on, the question is put by the chairman as to agreeing to or adopting the paper as amended, unless already adopted, as in such an instance as the revision of by-laws. But a report can be adopted, regardless

of any of the foregoing rules by general consent or
by suspending the rules.

If the amendments, as when reported from the committee of the whole, where they have been previously
discussed, do not call for debate or amendment, a
single question on all the committee's amendments
is put by the chairman, unless in case a member requests a separate vote by making a statement substantially as follows: "All those who are in favor
of adopting the amendments recommended by the
committee, except such amendments, which a separate
vote has been called for, will say aye; those not in
favor will say no." The remaining amendments will
then be taken up in order one at a time.

When a resolution with a substitute is reported back
by the committee, and which the committee recommends for adoption, the chairman states the question
on the substitute, providing that when the resolution
was committed there were no amendments pending.
However, if amendments were pending, then it is on
those pending amendments that the chairman first
states the questions, and then, after the amendments
have been disposed of, the question on the substitute
follows. In both instances the substitute is handled
in the same manner as any other substitute motion
would be, *i.e.*, first, the resolution is perfected by
amendments, and after that the substitute resolution.
When both have been perfected the question is put,
first on the substitution and then on the resolution,
which latter is open to amendment should the substitute be lost. No vote should be taken when the
report is of a nomination committee, the procedure
being just as though a member had made the nominations. When the report is from the membership committee the chairman proceeds immediately to state
the question as to the admission to membership of
candidates that the committee has recommended.

The partial and final reports of a committee are
treated alike. When a partial report refers only to
progress, and offers neither recommendations nor con-
clusions, it receives the same treatment given to any
other report of an informative nature, and does not
call for any action, unless it specifically recommends

action, in which instance the question is put on the adoption of the report, or its recommendations, or the resolutions, just as though the report were final.

Usually, in ordinary organizations, a motion to accept or adopt the report of a committee may be made and seconded. Should the motion not be made, the chairman may state the proper question, if he considers it best to have the question voted upon before any motion is made, assuming that the committee's submission of the report is tantamount to a move for the adoption of the proper motion for its disposal, as is done in cases where a resolution is offered.

The chairman of the assembly in ordinary organizations is, as a rule, more familiar with the manner of conducting the business than a reporting member, and particularly so when a resolution carrying with it many amendments is reported. In cases, however, where the chairman of an assembly has been in the habit, by tacit assent, of putting the appropriate questions on a report unaccompanied by a formal motion, it is preferable that the reporing member should move the "adoption" of the resolutions or recommendations; and the subject under consideration becomes open for debate and amendment as soon as the chairman has stated the question on the adoption of the resolutions or recommendations or of the report. Also, as with any main question, the subject being considered may have applied to it any of the subsidiary motions. There can be no objection opposed to the matter under consideration when it has been referred to the committee, and the assembly cannot in any particular alter or modify the report of the committee; although the report or resolutions of the committee are subject to amendments by the assembly, such amendments, however, affecting that only which the assembly adopts.

For instance, a committee condemns a certain act as objectionable, and this statement is struck out of the report by the assembly before it is adopted. In such case there is no alteration of the report; but just an adoption of the report by the assembly without this particular statement. Likewise, an assembly may strike out or add one or several resolutions or recommendations before adoption without altering the committee's report.

For publication the report of the committee should always be printed verbatim as it was submitted, with all words inserted printed in italics and all words struck out enclosed in brackets, with an explanatory note at the head of the document.

In the use of the words to "adopt," "accept," etc., where only one of the words is used, the word "adopt" should be given the preference, it being less likely than any other to be misconstrued.

Committee of the Whole

It is the practice to refer to the committee of the whole any business which comes up in the assembly for consideration when it is not deemed advisable to refer the subject matter to a committee.

In such cases a subject may be considered by the assembly without any restraint as in an ordinary committee and put in proper form for definite action, and if the consensus of opinion is that the question should have immediate consideration, a motion is made to that effect about as follows: "That the assembly now resolves itself into a committee of the whole to consider, etc.," or "that the assembly act as a committee of the whole to take under consideration, etc.," stating the subject to be considered.

If the motion is adopted and which is in reality a motion to commit, the chairman of the assembly becomes a member of the committee of the whole and another member takes his place as chairman. Excepting as hereinafter stated the committee is subject to the rules of the assembly.

As the committee cannot adjourn nor order the "yeas and nays," the motions to amend and adopt and that the committee "rise and report" are the only motions in order. If an appeal from the decision of the chair is made, it must be voted on immediately, and can neither be laid on the table nor postponed, as in a committee of the whole such motions are not permissible, and no member can speak more than once on an appeal.

When debate is to be closed or limited in a committee of the whole, the only procedure allowable is for the entire assembly to vote, before entering into committee, to limit the debate to a certain time, after which there shall be no debate permitted. The exception is to allow only one speech of about five minutes' duration in favor of, and one, limited to the same time, against any new amendments proposed; or some other practicable and permissible way to regulate the duration of debate may be employed.

When, however, no limit to debate has been drawn any member may consume as much time with his speech as would be allowed in the assembly, and he would be entitled to speak as often as he could get the floor, providing that no other member, who has not yet spoken on the question under debate, wants the floor.

When by the will of the assembly a debate has been closed at a given time, the committee is not empowered to extend the time even by unanimous consent. It cannot refer the subject to any other committee, nor can it alter the text of any resolution submitted to it, in which respect it is subject to the same inhibitions as are other committees. But where a resolution originates in the committee itself, then, and in that case, any or all amendments may be embodied in it.

The committee having concluded consideration of any matter which has been referred to it, or should it desire to have the debate limited by the assembly, or should it want to adjourn, some one moves that "the committee rise and report," i.e., state the result of the committee's work, etc.

Unless when a vote is in progress, or some member in the assembly has the floor, the committee's motion to "rise" is always in order, being of equal validity and privilege as a motion made in the assembly to adjourn, and which is neither debatable nor amendable.

When the motion to "rise" has been adopted, and the presiding officer has taken the chair, and the chairman of the committee has resumed his place in the assembly, he stands up and addresses the chair as follows:

"The committee of the whole has had under consideration (here the resolution or of whatever the business may have consisted is stated and explained) and said committee has instructed me to report the proceedings with the amendments (or without, should there not be any)."

Should the committee not have come to a conclusion, there should be written in the report "come to no conclusion thereon."

In the absence of any amendments, the question on the resolution, and other business referred to the committee, is immediately stated by the chairman. Should any amendments be reported, they are read by the reporting member, who then hands the paper to the chairman, who in turn reads it, states and puts the question on all of the amendments together. Should a separate vote be called for by any member on any one or several amendments then, all the other amendments are submitted singly to a vote, and the question is then stated on each amendment separately upon which a separate vote had been called for. The amendments then become debatable and amendable.

The quorum of an assembly and that of a committee of the whole are the same, and a committee, finding itself without a quorum, has no other alternative than to rise and report the deficiency to the assembly, which under such circumstances must adjourn.

The proceedings of a committee of the whole are not recorded in the minutes by the secretary; but a memorandum of the proceedings is usually filed for future reference and use. In assemblies of considerable numbers the chairman of the committee occupies the secretary's chair, which is vacated by the secretary for that purpose, and the assistant secretary fills the place as secretary of the committee.

In the event that a committee of the whole should get beyond the control of the chairman because of disorderly and tumultuous demonstrations, it becomes obligatory upon the presiding officer to take the chair and dissolve the committee.

Quasi Committee of the Whole

In small assemblies it is more convenient as a practice to use the Quasi Committee of the Whole, as, for instance, in the United States Senate, where it is used instead of the committee of the whole. In large assemblies, such as the House of Representatives, the use of the committee of the whole is almost indispensable, as a member cannot speak to any question more than once, and while permitting unrestrained discussion of a subject, can rise at any time and invoke the rigid rules of the assembly. The Quasi Committee of the Whole, also termed "as if in," is frequently made use of in other small bodies.

The usual form of motion to employ the "as if in" or Quasi Committee of the Whole is made somewhat as follows: "I move that the resolution be considered *as if in* committee of the whole. If the motion is adopted the question becomes debatable and amendable just as would occur in a committee of the whole.

In a quasi committee there is no chairman appointed as when the assembly becomes a committee of the whole, but the chairman of the assembly keeps the chair. With the exception of an amendment any motion adopted terminates the committee of the whole. Hence a motion to commit is tantamount to such motions in a committee of the whole as: (*a*) That the committee rise; (*b*) that from further consideration of the matter the committee of the whole be relieved; (*c*) and that the matter be referred to a committee. As soon as the assembly has completed the amendment of the proposition before it, the chairman announces, without further motion, that, acting as if in committee of the whole, the assembly has had under consideration such a matter and has made certain amendments, and he proceeds then to report them. The matter then comes before the assembly just as if the committee had made a report of it, and, as before explained, the chair states the question on the amendments. A memorandum of the proceedings should be kept by the secretary, just as though they had been executed in committee of the whole; but not being for permanent record they should not be recorded in the minutes. The chairman's report to the assembly, however, should be recorded in the minutes, as it pertains to the proceedings of the assembly.

Informal Consideration

In small assemblies of ordinary organizations the most frequent custom is to take the question under consideration informally rather than enter into committee of the whole, or to consider the questions as though they were in that committee. The motion to consider a question informally is usually stated substantially in this form: "I move the question be considered informally." Should the motion be adopted the effect is to open to free debate the main question and any proposed amendment, just as would occur in committee of the whole, and to the same question no member is permitted to speak the second time, when another member who has not spoken wants the floor. With the exception of the above informal consideration, and which has reference only to the main question and its amendments, all other motions that may be made are subject to the regular rules of debate. When a question is being considered informally, the number or length of speeches may be limited by a two-thirds vote of the assembly, or the debate limited or closed in any other permissible manner. All votes are formal, although the consideration of the main question and its amendments is informal and relates only to the number of speeches permitted in debate. When the informal consideration of the main question is for the time being or permanently disposed of, no motion or vote is required to effect its termination, as it ceases to exist automatically.

It is always necessary to report formally to the assembly, followed by action on the report, when a question is considered in either the regular or a Quasi Committee of the Whole, which renders an informal consideration much more simple than the manner of disposal previously described.

In small assemblies the use of this method has a decided advantage over the committee of the whole, ranking just below the motion "to consider as if in committee of the whole," which motion follows immediately in rank the motion "to go into committee of the whole."

CHAPTER XVI

Exemplar, Demonstrating the Proceedings of a Typical Society, or Association Meeting, in Actual Operation

Monthly Meeting of The Association of Amateur Athletes

Chairman (rises and taps the table with the gavel): "This meeting will now please come to order. What business is there to come before this meeting?"

Mr. Tucker (rises): "Mr. Chairman."

Chairman: "Mr. Tucker."

Mr. Tucker: "I move that overtures be made by this association to some professional athletic association, in good standing in this state, with a view to merging the two associations into one."

Mr. Miller (remaining seated): "I second the motion."

Chairman: "It has been moved and seconded, that overtures be made by this association to some professional athletic association, in good standing in this state, with a view to merging the two associations into one."

Mr. White (rises): "Mr. Chairman."

Chairman: "Mr. White."

Mr. White: "It would be more consistent for the members of our association to make a better showing in the amateur class before aspiring to rank as professionals."

Mr. Lansing (rises): "Mr. Chairman, I rise to a point of order." (*Mr. White resumes his seat and remains seated while point of order is being decided.*)

Chairman: "State your point."

Mr. Lansing: "My point of order is that it is a

distracting clement in the meeting for some members in the rear of the hall to be constantly opening and shutting the main entrance door.''

Chairman: ''The point of order is well taken. Members in the rear will please discontinue needlessly opening and shutting the main entrance door. Mr. White has the floor.''

Mr. White (rises): ''It is very doubtful if any professional association would consider a merger with an association of raw amateurs with a record none too brilliant.''

Mr. King (rises): ''From my point of view—''

Chairman (interrupting): ''Mr. King you are out of order. You did not address the chair and you have not been recognized.''

Mr. King: ''Beg pardon, Mr. Chairman, my omission was unintentional.''

Chairman: ''Mr. King.''

Mr. King: ''From my point of view, it will require at least three years of practice in every line of athletics, and much hard work, before we should entertain any idea of entering the professional field.''

Mr. Bowles (rises): ''Mr. Chairman.''

Chairman: ''Mr. Bowles.''

Mr. Bowles: ''I move to amend the motion by inserting the words 'some time during the year of 1965' after the words 'that overtures be made by this association.' ''

Mr. Blake (does not rise or address the chair): ''I second the motion.''

Chairman: ''It has been moved and seconded to amend the motion by inserting the words, 'some time during the year of 1965,' after the words, 'that overtures be made by this association,' so that the motion, if amended, would read, 'that overtures be made by this association, some time during the year of 1965, to some professional athletic association, in good standing in this state, with a view to merging the two associations into one.' Is there any discussion on the amendment?''

Mr. Stokes (rises): ''Mr. Chairman, I rise to a point of information.''

Chairman: ''State your question.''

Mr. Stokes: "In what month in the year 1965 is it proposed to make the overtures to some professional athletic association, as referred to in the motion?"

Chairman (addressing Mr. Butler): "Can you inform him?"

Mr. Butler (rises): "It seems to me that the month is immaterial. Any month to be decided upon hereafter should be suitable."

Chairman: "If the amendment is not to be discussed further, the vote* will now be taken on it."

Mr. Parker and **Mr. King** (rise together): "Mr. Chairman."

Chairman: "Mr. Parker."

Mr. King (standing): "Mr. Chairman, I rise to a point of order."

Chairman: "State your point."

Mr. King: "My point of order is, Why was I not recognized when I addressed the chair precisely at the same moment as the speaker?"

Chairman: "Because it is an established custom to recognize a member who has not spoken in preference to one who has. You will have the floor after Mr. Parker."

Mr. Parker (rises): "I move to amend the amendment by striking out the words 'some time during the year of 1965,' and inserting in their place the words 'in the month of January, 1966.'"

Chairman: "Who seconds the motion?" (No response being made, the chairman declares): "The motion is lost for want of a second."

Mr. Allen (rises): "Mr. Chairman."

Chairman: "Mr. Allen."

Mr. Allen: "In my judgment I think that the members of our association would derive more material benefit and acquire more versatility in athletic skill if the members of the various teams were interchanged oftener and—"

Chairman: (interrupting): "Mr. Allen, you are out of order, because you are not confining your discus-

* When putting a motion to a vote the chairman should stand, and remain standing, or take his seat during the remainder of the time, as the size and formality of the assembly may suggest.

sion to the matter pending, and which is the amendment to add to the main motion the words 'some time during the year of 1965.' ''

Mr. Allen (rises again): ''I think the chairman entertains a wrong impression. I was speaking on the subject—''

Chairman: ''Asking your pardon, Mr. Allen, I would inform you that no member is permitted to argue with the chairman as to his decision on a point of order.'' (Addressing the assembly the chairman continues): ''Is the amendment to be discussed further? If not, all those in favor of the amendment, which is that the words 'some time during the year of 1965' be added to the main motion, say, 'aye.' ''

(The chairman declares the amendment carried.)

Mr. Davis (rises): ''Mr. Chairman, I rise to a point of order.''

Chairman: ''State your point.''

Mr. Davis: ''My point of order is that the chair did not call for the negative vote.''

Chairman: ''Your point is well taken, and the chair stands corrected. All those in favor of the amendment say 'aye.' Those not in favor say 'no.' The amendment is carried, and the motion as amended now reads: 'that overtures be made by this association, some time during the year of 1965, to some professional athletic association, in good standing in this state, with a view to merging the two associations into one.' Is there any discussion on the motion as amended? If not, all those in favor of the motion say 'aye.' Those not in favor say 'no.' The motion is carried.''

Mr. Sterling (rises): ''Mr. Chairman.''

Chairman: ''Mr. Member.''

Mr. Sterling: ''I move that this association adopt some distinctive emblem to be conspicuously displayed on all working attire used by the members.''

Mr. Bradley (remaining seated): ''I second the motion.''

Chairman (restating the motion): ''It has been moved and seconded, that this association adopt some distinctive emblem, to be conspicuously displayed on all working attire used by the members. Is there any discussion?'' (Chairman waits a few moments for response. Being no response, the chairman continues): ''If there is no further discussion, all those in favor of the motion say *'aye.'* Those opposed say *'no.'* The motion is carried and the distinctive emblem mentioned in the motion shall be adopted.''

Mr. Bromley (rises): ''Mr. Chairman.''

Chairman: ''Mr. Bromley.''

Mr. Bromley: ''I move that we do not give our annual ball this year.''

Chairman: ''Please state your motion in the affirmative. A negative motion is sometimes confusing to members when voting.''

Mr. Bromley: ''I move that we dispense with our annual ball this year.''

Mr. Harvey (remaining seated): ''I second the motion.''

Chairman: ''It has been moved and seconded that we dispense with our annual ball this year. Is there any discussion? If not all those in favor of the motion say *'aye.'* Those opposed say *'no.'* The motion is carried and we shall dispense with our annual ball this year.''

Mr. Whipple (rises): ''Mr. Chairman.''

Chairman: ''Mr. Whipple.''

Mr. Whipple: ''I move that we adjourn.''

Mr. Tindel: ''I second the motion.''

Chairman: ''It has been moved and seconded to adjourn. All those in favor say *'aye.'* Those opposed say *'no.'* The motion is carried and the meeting adjourned.''

Of Meetings

Mass Meeting

The preliminary steps that should be taken before calling a meeting, which is not one of a permanent organization, are as follows: ''The promoters of the meeting should decide (a) upon the time and place of the meeting (*b*) the manner in which notice of it should be given, (*c*) by whom it shall be called to order, and the chairman nominated, and who shall the chairman be, and who shall state the object of the meeting to the assemblage and submit any resolutions that may have been prepared for that purpose.

It is usual to call a mass meeting to order, by whomever may have been selected for the purpose, in the following manner:

First Member (selected to call meeting to order, stepping to the front): "The meeting will please come to order. **I move** that Mr. X be made chairman of this meeting, [or, **I nominate** Mr. X for chairman of this meeting]."

Second Member (any member): "I second the motion [or nomination]."

First Member: "It has been moved and seconded that Mr. X be made chairman of this meeting, [or, Mr. X has been nominated for chairman of this meeting]. All those in favor of the motion [or nomination) say '*aye.*' Those opposed say '*no.*' (The vote being counted and showing a majority voting '*aye,*' he continues): The '*ayes*' have it and Mr. X is elected chairman."

Should the motion be lost, someone else is proposed for chairman, and the same procedure is repeated until a chairman is elected.

Sometimes the member who is elected to call the meeting to order acts as temporary chairman himself, and after calling the meeting to order, will ask that someone nominate a chairman, and this being done he puts the question to vote as shown above, saying: "Will someone nominate a chairman, etc."

When the chairman is elected and is conducted to the chair (usually by the nominating member and one other member in large assemblies) he says: "The election of a secretary is the first business in order"; and unless someone else makes a motion, he continues "I nominate Mr. X," and then the question is put in the usual way as before described. If, however, more than one name is called out from members of the assembly, the chairman, in the order in which the names were called, in so far as he can distinguish, says: "Mr.

Y is nominated, or Mr. Z is nominated—and so on, as he happens to have retained all the names in his memory—and he then puts the question to vote, on the first name he heard, in the usual manner, *i. e.,* "All those in favor of Mr. Y for secretary say *'aye.'* Those opposed say *'no.'*" Should there be any uncertainty in the mind of the chairman as to the preponderance of the vote one way or the other, the chairman will call for those in favor of Mr. Y to rise and for those opposed to rise. Seeing that the opposition is manifestly stronger than those in favor, he says: "The negative has it and the motion is lost." Continuing, he says: "Those who are in favor of Mr. Z for secretary say *'aye'*; those opposed say *'no.'* The *'ayes'* have it and Mr. Z is elected secretary. Mr. Z will please take his place at the desk."

Should Mr. Z not be elected the voting is continued in the order of the nominations until one is elected.

In all large assemblies the chairman should stand in putting the question to vote, and the secretary should be seated nearby and keep a record of the proceedings. It is optional whether or not nominations are seconded, and ordinarily there is no debate, though it is permissible, and not unusual, for the member who makes the nomination, or the one who seconds it, or both, to make a few remarks complimentary to their nominee. A nomination is not amendable; and any officers in addition to a secretary that may be required are elected by the same procedure.

Adoption of Resolutions

The chairman and secretary having been elected, all that is necessary to proceed with the business of a meeting has been effected.

The chairman begins by directing the secretary to read the call for the meeting and then calls upon the member most qualified for the purpose, to explain the object of the meeting, so that it may be thoroughly understood by all present.

This may be done by the chairman himself, if in his judgment it is more expedient or convenient.

After the explanation is made someone moves that

a committee be appointed to draw up resolutions upon the subject; or a series of resolutions may be offered that have already been drawn.

The procedure at this juncture is substantially as follows:

A Member (presenting solutions already prepared): "Mr. Chairman."

Chairman: "Mr. Member."

A Member: "I move the adoption of the following resolutions." [*The member then reads the resolutions and hands them to the chairman.*]

Another Member: "I second the motion."

Chairman: "It has been moved and seconded to adopt the following resolutions." [*Here the chairman reads the resolutions or directs the secretary to do so.*] Continuing, he says: "The question is on the adoption of the resolutions [*no one rising at once*], are you ready for the question*?"

[*The debate, if any, being closed, the chairman says:*] "Are you ready for the question?" [*No one rising, he continues*]: "All those in favor of the adoption of the resolutions say 'aye,'" [*The 'ayes' having voted, he continues*]: "All those who are opposed say 'no.'" [*The affirmative vote being in preponderance, he continues*]: "The motion is carried (or the 'ayes' have it), and the resolutions are adopted."

Division of Resolutions

When several resolutions referring to different subjects are reported by the committee, and a single member should make the request, the chair must state the question on the resolutions separately. Resolutions referring to a single subject, and where each one can stand alone, notwithstanding the rejection of the others, may be divided by a majority vote on a motion to divide the question. However, under conditions where they cannot stand alone, the right procedure to get a separate vote on an undesirable resolution,

---

* At this juncture the resolutions are open to debate and amendment. They may be referred to committee, or any other subsidiary motion may be applied to them.

is a motion to strike it out; but this motion is open to amendment in order to get it in most advantageous shape before the vote is taken on it.

Amending a Resolution

To amend a resolution which has been placed before the assembly for action by the chairman, or one that is pending, some member, obtaining the floor, moves that the resolution be amended by, for instance, inserting a certain word after one contained in the resolution. If the motion is not immediately seconded, the chairman says: "Has the motion been seconded?" Usually repeating the motion in order to be sure that it has been heard by the whole assembly. When the motion is seconded the chairman continues as follows: "It is moved and seconded [*stating the amendment verbatim*]; are you ready for the question?" At this juncture, the question becomes what is known as the *"immediately pending question,"* and is open to debate and amendment, having superseded the resolution. In the absence of any member now rising and obtaining the floor the chairman says: "As many of those [*or all those*] in favor of the amendment [or motion] say 'aye,' those opposed [*or not in favor*] say 'no.'" If the number of affirmative votes predominate, the chairman announces: "The 'ayes' have it and the amendment is adopted. The question is now on the resolution as amended." [*The chairman here states the resolution as amended.*] Continuing, the chairman asks: "Are you ready for the question?" The resolution is now again the *"immediate pending question"* and is open to debate and amendment. If there is no debate, or if the debate has come to a close, the chairman asks: "Are you ready for the question?" Should no member rise to claim the floor the chairman continues, putting the question as follows: "The question is on adopting the following resolution. 'Resolved,' [*here the chairman reads or states the resolution*]. Those in favor of adopting the resolution [*or, of the motion*] say 'aye'; those opposed say 'no.' The 'ayes' have it and the resolution is adopted."

Committee to Draft Resolutions

When it is desirable to appoint a committee to draft resolutions, some member makes a motion that a committee [*stating of how many the committee should be composed*] be appointed by the chair to draft resolutions indicative of the sense of this meeting, and he states the purpose for which the meeting was called. Then the formula of seconding the motion, etc., is followed, as above described, and the question is put to the vote. When the motion is adopted, the chairman appoints the committee (of whatever the number may be) on resolutions and instructs them to withdraw and prepare the resolutions with as little delay as possible. This the committee does, and when they agree upon a report (which should be written) they return to the room. Meanwhile any other business before the assembly may be taken up or attention given to addresses from members. As soon as the committee returns to the room, and pending business is disposed of, and any member who may be speaking at the time has finished his speech, the chairman announces that the report of the committee on resolutions will now be heard by the assembly. If the return of the committee to the room has not been observed by the chairman of the assembly, it is incumbent upon the chairman of the committee to obtain the floor and inform the assembly (addressing the chair) that the committee is prepared to make the report. The chairman of the assembly replies that the report will be heard, and then the chairman of the committee proceeds to read it, and immediately upon concluding the reading he moves its adoption and hands it to the chairman of the assembly, which procedure automatically dissolves the committee. Then follows the same routine as above described until the resolutions are adopted; or they may be debated, amended, or consideration of them postponed.

After all the business for which the assembly was convened has been disposed of, or for any other reason it is neither necessary nor desirable to prolong the meeting, a motion is made by some one *"to adjourn"*;

but this motion, like any other main motion, may be debated and amended, unless no time has been set for another meeting, in which case—the motion being carried—the chairman announces that the vote is in the affirmative and the assembly stands adjourned *"Sine die"* (without day).

But when a time for an adjourned meeting has been set, the chairman announces that the assembly has been adjourned to whatever the appointed time may be.

Semi-permanent Mass Meeting

This plan of a meeting is sometimes chosen when one meeting does not suffice to accomplish the object for which the assembly is convened, and it best serves the purposes to make at first a temporary organization and work it into a semi-permanent organization by feasible stages. When this plan is adopted the procedure for organization is the same as above described except that the qualifying prefix *"pro tem"* is given to the titles of the officers, and yet never used in addressing them. Just as above described in the case of a mass meeting (or convention), as soon as the *"pro tem"* secretary is elected, a committee is appointed to nominate the semi-permanent officers. Such matters as the time and place for holding meetings; the restriction of speeches as to number, duration, etc.; the establishment of some authority on parliamentary law, etc., are committed to a committee on rules.

In large, formal meetings the presiding officer is the president, and the vice-presidents—often quite numerous in large meetings—occupy the platform with and alongside of him, and the highest on the list of the vice-presidents always takes the chair in the absence of the president.

A Permanent Society

The initial steps in the formation of a permanent society are, *(a)* for the promoters to have thoroughly laid their plans, and *(b)* to have categorically outlined their objects and purposes, and *(c)* to have assured themselves of the sympathy and support of

a majority of the prospective members, before calling
a meeting to organize. Having taken all the preliminary steps as described in the organization of a mass
meeting (see "Mass Meeting," page 157) they should
notify those whom they have reason to think are interested in the objects for which the society is proposed to be instituted, to meet at a given time and
place to take the project contemplated under consideration and perfect a suitable constitution and
such appropriate by-laws as are usually adopted by
similar societies.

When the meeting to organize a society is convened,
as in a mass meeting, some one, to whom the office has
been previously assigned, steps to the front and calls
the meeting to order, and then makes a motion that
someone (*naming the person*) act as chairman of
the meeting. This motion being seconded by someone,
the maker of the motion puts the question (*i.e., puts
it to vote*) in the manner elsewhere described (see
"Mass Meeting," page 157). When the chairman is
elected and takes the chair, and the election of a secretary follows, as in a mass meeting, the chairman
then calls upon one of the principal promoters interested in the formation of the society to state the object
of the meeting. The chairman may also call for the
views of other members upon the subject, maintaining
consistently a reasonable measure of restraint upon
speakers inclined to unnecessary and tiresome ver-
bosity, while at the same time exercising good judgment in the execution of his principal official function,
which is to yield literally and in spirit to the wishes
of the assembly.

The next step in the process of organization is the
offering by someone of a resolution upon some definite action—and this usually has been preconceived,
agreed upon, and prepared in the form of a suitable
resolution to be offered at a proper stage of the proceedings. Such a resolution usually takes a form substantially as follows: "*Resolved,* That the consensus
of opinion and sense of this meeting is that a society
be formed in this state for (*here the object or objects
of the society should be specifically stated*)."

After this resolution has been seconded and stated

by the chair—it being open to debate and amendment —it is treated in the same manner, and follows the same course, as that described on page 157 under "Mass Meeting."

In very large meetings, however, much time may be saved, with satisfactory results, by offering the preliminary motion at the opening of the meeting, thereby eliminating unimportant informal discussion. A shorter cut to quick and efficient procedure, in a large assembly, is to offer a motion at the very outset that the chairman appoint a committee of (*stating the number constituting committee*) to draft a constitution and by-laws for a society for (*stating the object, etc., of the society*) and that said committee make its report at an adjourned meeting. This motion is debatable, amendable by striking out and adding words.

This committee being appointed, and the chairman having asked the assembly whether any other business requires attention, and there is nothing further to be done, a motion is then appropriate to adjourn to a specified time and place. This motion is open to debate and amendment after it is seconded and stated by the chairman. However, if the matter of time and place of the next meeting is first settled at an earlier stage of the proceedings, and later on a motion is made simply "to adjourn," without any reference or specification as to time and place, such motion cannot be amended or debated, and the chairman announces that the meeting "stands adjourned," to meet at the time and place previously fixed.

When the next meeting is held, those officers, if present, who acted at the first meeting continue to officiate until the permanent ones are elected. After the chairman (*standing*) has called this meeting to order, and the assembly is seated, he directs the secretary to read the minutes of the last meeting and then takes his seat. When the secretary has finished reading the minutes, and anyone thinks an error is contained in them, and wants a correction made, he should state the fact at once. Then the chairman, in the absence of any objection, and without waiting for a motion, directs the secretary to make the correction, which being done, the chairman announces to the assembly that "the minutes stand approved as read [*or as corrected*]."

At this juncture the chairman announces that the report of the committee on the constitution and by-laws will be heard, as being the next business in order before the assembly. Then the chairman of the committee, addressing the chairman of the assembly, and after being recognized, makes a statement substantially as follows: ".The committee appointed to draft a constitution and by-laws, having agreed upon the contents of this report, has directed me to submit it to the assembly and move its adoption." The chairman of the committee, after reading the report and making a motion for its adoption, hands it to the chair.

After the motion has been seconded, and the chairman announces that it has been moved and seconded to adopt the constitution and by-laws reported by the committee, he continues: "The question is on the adoption of the constitution which will now be read." This is done from the platform, either by the secretary or the chairman of the committee, as the chair may elect. (*This second reading is not often considered worthwhile, and by general concurrence is omitted.*) Then, the first paragraph of the report, and the succeeding ones in turn, are read by the chairman, or by whomever he may direct to do so, and he asks if there are any amendments proposed to the paragraphs which he reads in the order in which they appear in the report.

If on any paragraph, as they are read in consecutive order, there are any amendments offered, these are disposed of in the usual manner, and when no further amendments are forthcoming, and the chairman thinks that the constitution has been amended in form to meet with the approval of the assembly, he puts the question on the constitution amended as a whole, as no vote may be taken on any amendment of a separate paragraph; because the chairman has gone through the entire constitution, paragraph at a time, and reduced the question to the whole, which embodies all particulars. When this stage of the proceedings has been reached, and which is the proper time to introduce additional paragraphs or offer amendments, and none are forthcoming, the chairman says: "Are you ready for the question?" No one answering, he continues: "All those in favor of adopting the constitution as amended say 'aye'; those not in favor [or, opposed] say 'no.'" He then announces the result of the vote, which to adopt a constitution for a new society is only necessary to show a majority. Following this proceeding, and when the assembly is large, a short recess is usually taken upon a motion in order to enable those wishing to become members to sign the constitution and comply with such other of its requirements, if any, as, for instance, the payment of initiation fees, etc.

After the recess the chairman calls the meeting to order and directs the secretary to read the roll of members, as these only will be qualified to participate in the future proceedings of the organization. Then the question on the adoption of the by-laws reported by the committee comes before the assembly and the chairman directs the secretary to read them. This being done, the proceedings, as in the case of the constitution, are repeated. No further motion is now required, as the motion to adopt the constitution and by-laws reported by the committee has already been made when the committee made its report.

Following the adoption of the by-laws the next business in order is the election of the permanent officers. The method of their nomination and election should be contained in the by-laws and acted upon in accordance therewith. Should no such provision for the nomination and election of these officers be embodied in the by-laws, it becomes incumbent upon the chairman to inquire of the assembly how the officers shall be nominated. Then a motion may be made and adopted that the chair appoint a committee to make the nominations, which the chairman proceeds to do, and the committee then retires and makes up the ticket. While the committee is engaged in agreeing upon a ticket, any other business that happens to be pending may be given attention, or the assembly may take a recess. When the committee returns to the room, and all pending business being disposed of, the chairman of the assembly calls for the committee's report which is handed to him by the chairman of the committee after he has read aloud the list of nominations. Then the list is read by the chairman, after which he says substantially as follows: "Are there any other names to be put in nomination?" or, "Are there any more nominations to be made?" In response to the chairman's inquiry any member may rise, address the chair, and after being recognized, place anyone else in nomination for any office, or he may propose an entirely new ticket by nominating a different person for each office. This modified or wholly new ticket is announced by the chairman, and after waiting a few moments, and glancing around the assembly, he asks: "Are there any further nominations?" If no further names are offered in nomination, the chairman proceeds to have the vote taken—which is usually by ballot in conformity with the by-laws of most organizations—and the tellers who are appointed move around through the assembly, by direction of the chairman, distributing blank ballots to the members, upon which they write the names of their choice of the nominees standing for each office. After being filled out by the members the chairman directs the tellers to collect them, and after assuring himself that all have voted, he announces that "the polls are closed," and instructs the tellers to count the ballots. When this has been done, the result of the count is reported to the chairman by the teller who was first appointed. The chairman then announces to the assembly as elected such candidates as have received a majority vote, and the announcement of the election of these permanent officers does away automatically with the temporary ones.

The president, if elected on the first ballot, takes the chair immediately, and should any of the offices not have been filled, blank ballots are again distributed by order of the chairman, and the assembly is directed to fill them in with the names of their choice for the unfilled offices. This procedure of balloting repeatedly is continued until all of the permanent offices are filled.

Unless declared ineligible by the by-laws, any member may be voted for, whether or not he is a nominee.

Sometimes, because of the lateness of the hour, or for some other cause, it becomes necessary to adjourn a meeting before the completion of organization can be effected and the regular work of the society begun, such as the appointment of committees for various purposes, etc.

Under such circumstances, and after an adjourned meeting has been provided for, some member should make a motion to adjourn, which motion being carried, the chairman announces the vote and declares the meeting adjourned. In order that no member may be left in uncertainty as to the previously established and known time and place for the next meeting, it is advisable that the chairman should make mention of the time and place when declaring the adjournment.

Regular Business Meetings of a Permanent Society

The regular business meetings of a permanent society, after it has been thoroughly organized, are conducted in the following manner: At the regularly fixed hour for the opening of the meeting the presiding officer calls the meeting to order from the chair and then directs the minutes of the last meeting be read by the secretary. When the secretary has finished reading the minutes, the chairman asks the assembly if there are any corrections to be made in them. None being suggested, he says: "No corrections being suggested, the minutes stand approved as read." Should any corrections be suggested, and there is no opposition, they are made by the secretary. If, however, some one moves to amend the minutes the chairman may put the question on the amendment offered, or he may even put the question on a suggestion of amendment without waiting for a motion to be made.

When the matter of any proposed amendment is disposed of, and there is no response to his inquiry: "Are there any more corrections (or amendments) to the minutes?" he continues: "There being no more corrections (or amendments) suggested for the minutes, they now stand approved as corrected." The chairman then submits to the assembly the next business in order as prescribed by the rules of the society.

If the order of business* is that which is usually followed by permanent societies, as soon as the minutes are read and approved, the chairman says: "The next business in order is hearing the reports of the standing committees." He may then call for the report of each committee in its order, asking: "Has the committee on [*here the name of the committee is stated*] any report to make?" Or, he may make the inquiry of the several committees as if of one, thus: "Have the committees any reports to make?" If no one rises to report, the chairman continues: "The standing committees having no reports to make, the business next in order is hearing the reports of special committees." The same procedure is then followed as in the case of the standing committees. The chairman then proceeds to the next business in order and so continues throughout the list until all the business of the meeting has been concluded. At this juncture a motion is made by someone to adjourn, and if the motion is carried, the chairman announces the vote and declares the meeting adjourned.

An Organized Convention
Composed of Authorized Delegates

An organized convention which has a constitution, by-laws, and officers when convened, should have a committee on credentials, or registration, and one on program. Such committees are usually appointed previous to the meeting, either at a previous convention, or by the president, or by an executive board in consonance with the by-laws. The committee on credentials or registration should have its report ready and be prepared to submit it immediately after the opening speeches have been made. It is advisable that the committee should be present at the place of meeting, or

* When no rule has been adopted, it is customary for permanent societies to adopt a regular order of business for its meetings, viz.: (1) Reading the Minutes of the previous meeting [and their approval]. (2) Reports of Boards and Standing Committees. (3) Reports of Special (Select) Committees. (4) Special Orders. (5) Unfinished Business and General Orders. (6) New Business.

at some previously selected headquarters at a reasonable time before the meeting is to be opened, to attend to the registration of the delegates and furnish them with some evidence of their right of admission to the place of meeting, and which is usually provided for in the form of cards or badges. It is also a good idea, and greatly facilitates the successful handling of a large body of delegates, that the committee on program should be well supplied in advance with programs, and the constituent bodies be amply supplied in order that all the delegates may be provided with one and have ample time and opportunity to familiarize themselves with the working schedules of the convention and the various arrangements made by the local committees, for their comfort and entertainment.

Usually large conventions—and particularly political ones—are attended by much confusion and boisterous enthusiasm, when the crowd first gathers in the convention hall and before the assembly is called to order, so that oftentimes the tact and cool resourcefulness of a presiding officer is strained almost to the limit in his efforts to check the general disorder and get the attention of the assemblage when the hour is at hand to call the convention to order. When the presiding officer has succeeded, with the aid of his gavel, in attracting attention, he calls out: "The convention will come to order." When the convention comes to order, some form of opening exercise, appropriate to the character of the convention, is gone through with, and then the presiding officer begins with the order of business as prescribed in the program, although the program may not yet have been adopted by the convention. The provisions contained in the program for the order of business in a large convention after the opening exercises are over usually are: The hearing of the report of the committee on credentials so that it may be known what persons present are entitled to vote, and this report is in the form of a list containing the names of the registered delegates and their alternates, if any, whose credentials have been accepted and approved, and also the names of the ex-officio members of the convention who have registered as present.

Ex-officio members of a convention, as the constitution does or should provide, are: The officers of the convention who are present, the chairmen of the different committees that make reports to the convention, and the members of the Board of Managers. All reports made to a convention should be read from the platform, either by the chairman of the committee, or the reading secretary, or official reader.

Sometimes a contest arises between two bodies of delegates as to which is entitled to recognition, and in such case neither delegation is entered in the list; but the fact of the contest is reported by the committee. The names of legitimate delegates—*i.e.*, where their claims to recognition are evidently valid—are entered on the list, regardless of any contest, and no one can vote unless his name is contained in the list reported by the committee. Neither one of any two delegations can vote upon a motion to substitute one for the other; and such persons only, whose names are contained in the list of members reported by the committee, and amended by the convention, are entitled to vote upon the main motion to accept the report.

Following the adoption of the credential committee's report, the president proceeds to call for the program committee's report, and the chairman of that committee submits the printed program and makes a motion that it be adopted; or, someone else may move its adoption. This motion is open to debate and amendment, but cannot be amended again after it has been adopted by a majority vote, except by a majority vote of the entire membership, or a two-thirds vote of those voting.

After the details of membership and program have been disposed of, the business next in order, as specified in the program, is taken up and conducted according to the usual parliamentary routine as heretofore described. The two principal committees (committee on credentials and committee on program) are continued throughout the session, as supplementary duties may be required of them, as, for instance, the arrival of additional delegates, or the failure of certain speakers to appear, or for other reasons necessitating changes in the program which should be reported at any time as additional reports, in conformity, however, as far as possible with the provisions of the program as originally adopted.

In an organized convention annual reports are required to be made and submitted by the treasurer, standing committees and boards, and from other officers when considered necessary. The term of office for the officers, board of managers, etc., is for two years, as prescribed in some constitutions, but the more general custom is to elect them annually, and it is often deemed advisable to elect only one-half of the officers at any one annual meeting. When the session of a convention extends—as they most always do—over a number of days, it is the practice to read the minutes of the preceding day and have them approved before proceeding to the business of the present day. However, in some instances, as, for instance, at the close of a convention, when there may not be time, or conditions are not favorable to read the minutes of the last day, the minutes for that day may, upon an adopted motion, be approved by the board or some committee thus authorized to act.

When all the business before the convention has been disposed of, it adjourns *sine die* (without day).

A Convention Not Organized

A convention not yet organized has no constitution, by-laws, or officers when called to order. Differing from a ''Mass Meeting,'' as described on page 157, it is presented with the problem of ascertaining who is entitled to vote; but in other respects it is similar.

Note.—The following model form of constitution and by-laws, with such modifications as may be suggested by the nature and objects of various societies, associations, clubs, etc., may be made to apply to organizations in general.

Constitution and By-Laws for an Association for the Promotion of Arts and Letters

Constitution

Preamble

With the object in view of stimulating a greater interest and development in the arts and letters in our city and state, and creating an enthusiasm which, by reason of our example, will serve to awaken a spirit of emulation and co-operation to the same end throughout the nation, we do hereby form ourselves into the Boston Association for the Promotion of Arts and Letters.

Consonant with the most liberal spirit of tolerance in the achievement of our purpose, we further agree that in its vigorous pursuit, this organization shall at all times during the span of its existence, maintain an attitude strictly non-sectarian, non-partisan and non-sectional, nor shall it, as an organization, take any part in political issues, or the affairs of state.

Article I

Name

The Boston Association for the Promotion of Arts and Letters shall be the name of this organization.

Article II

Membership

Section 1. All citizens who are interested in the promotion of arts and letters are eligible to membership in this association.

174

Section 2. Pursuant to the process provided in the by-laws, persons of notable ability, and who are in sympathy with the objects of this association, may have honorary membership conferred upon them.

Article III

Officers

A president, a first and second vice-president, a secretary, and a treasurer shall constitute the official personnel of this organization, and their terms of office shall be for one year.

Article IV

Board of Directors

There shall be vested in a board of eleven directors the authority to govern this organization, by directing its policy and operations in all matters relating to the objects for which it has been formed.

Article V

Meetings

Section 1. On the third Tuesday in May of each year the annual meeting of this organization shall be held.

Section 2. Not less than one regular meeting shall be held every two months, and power shall be vested in the board of directors to fix the date of such meetings.

Section 3. Upon the written request of eight members of this organization, or whenever deemed desirable by the board of directors, special meetings shall be called.

Article VI

If an amendment to this constitution should be proposed at any regular meeting of this organization, it may be made, if carried, by a three-fourths vote of those voting; provided, however, that the proposed amendment has been previously approved of by the board of directors, and their approval has been posted on the bulletin board, and the same information also mailed by the secretary to each member at least one week before the vote is taken.

By-Laws

Membership

Section 1. To attain actual membership the procedure as follows shall be observed:

The candidate's written application shall be submitted to the board of directors not less than one week before the vote upon his name is taken, and during that period a notice shall be mailed by the secretary to each member of the board informing him of the candidate's application. The names of all candidates for membership shall be read and voted upon at each regular meeting of the board.

Section 2. The manner of conferring honorary membership shall be as follows: To the membership committee must be submitted in writing the proposal to confer honorary membership, and, in turn, this committee shall submit in writing to the board of directors the name of the person upon whom honorary membership is to be conferred, and state the reasons therefor. This procedure is effective unless opposed by more than one member of the committee, and unless opposed by more than two negative votes from the board of directors, announcement of approval of the candidate shall be posted on the bulletin board for ten days, and any objection made by members must be made to the board before the expiration of this time. All elections to honorary membership shall be announced at the following regular meeting of this organization.

Section 3. Payment of dues shall not be required of honorary members, and they shall be granted all the privileges of membership with the exception of voting or holding office.

Section 4. Twenty-five dollars ($25) shall be payable on the first day of May, the annual dues of membership in this organization, and members elected at different times during the year shall pay *pro rata* for intervening time between date of election and the first day of May.

Section 5. Any member who becomes delinquent for a period of sixty days shall have his name posted on the bulletin board for one week after having been notified of his delinquency in writing by the treasurer; and should he continue delinquent after the expiration of this time, his membership shall be declared forfeited by the board of directors.

Officers

Section 6. The president shall be a member, ex-officio, of all committees.

Section 7. The secretaryship shall be a salaried office, the amount of compensation to be fixed by the board of directors. The duties of the secretary shall be the handling of all official correspondence, filing all records and communications, and the recording of all the proceedings of the board of directors and those of all committees, and all the business in general that comes before and is disposed of by this organization. He shall give bond in an amount to be determined by the board of directors, and he shall act as a member, ex-officio, of all committees.

Section 8. The treasurer shall give a bond the amount of which shall be determined by the board of directors.

The Board of Directors

Section 9. The board of directors shall elect from amongst themselves, within a week after their own election, the following officers, *viz.*, president, first and second vice-president, secretary, and a treasurer. The secretary shall be a salaried officer and his compensation shall be fixed by the board, of which he himself becomes a member upon election, but without the privilege of voting. The office of president of the board of directors shall be filled by the president of the organization. Power shall be vested in the board of directors to take whatever action they may deem necessary or advisable for the government and direction of this organization. They shall formulate and adopt rules for the conducting of business, for the filling of vacancies on the board, and for the management and control of the property of this organization. Complete reports of all actions and decisions shall be submitted by the secretary at each of the annual meetings.

Resignations

Section 10. All resignations shall be made in writing and presented to the board of directors; but no resignation shall cancel the dues of a member for that part of the fiscal year during which he has had the privileges of membership.

Expulsion

Section 11. Any member whose expulsion has been proposed, and may be effected by a two-thirds vote of the whole board of directors, is entitled to a personal hearing before the board, but without the right of representation by outside counsel. Before any proceedings are taken in the proposed expulsion of a member he must have written notice of the contemplated action.

Committees

Section 12. All committees shall be appointed by the president of this organization, subject to the approval of the board of directors; and all routine business shall be transacted by a committee composed of seven members. This committee shall be empowered to act for the board when it is not in session between meetings: to make disbursements, fix salaries, etc.; and all business transacted by this committee shall be submitted by the president of this organization to the board of directors for confirmation.

Section 13. An auditing committee, none of whom

shall be members of the board of directors, shall be
appointed by the president subject to the approval
of the members of this organization, at a meeting preceding immediately every annual meeting, and all
the accounts of the treasurer, secretary, board of
directors, and of all committees shall be audited by
this committee and a report made to the organization
at the annual meeting.

Elections

Section 14. The election of a board of directors
shall take place annually on the first Monday in May,
and the members of the nominating committee shall
be nominated from the floor, and voted upon by ballot
at the last regular meeting prior to the annual meeting.
The five candidates receiving the greatest number of
votes are elected.

Each member of the organization shall have sent
to him, seven days prior to the election, a special notice
of this meeting, with a list of twenty-five candidates
prepared by the nominating committee and posted on
the bulletin board. Or, a board of directors may be
nominated by any twenty members by posting a list
on the bulletin board over their signatures one week
before the election.

Section 15. A committee of five tellers, who are not
members of the board of directors, or candidates for
that position, shall be appointed by the president at
the last annual meeting prior to the election, and
these five tellers shall conduct the election.

Disbursements

Section 16. All disbursements must be ordered and
approved by the executive committee and board of directors, signed by the secretary or president and pay-
ments made by check. Only by the unanimous vote of
the directors, or by a five-sixths vote of the members
in attendance at any regular meeting of this organization, shall any appropriation of money, or disposition of property be made.

Parliamentary Authority

Section 17. This organization shall be governed in all its meetings by parliamentary law as contained in MODERN RULES OF ORDER, published by Fawcett Publications, Inc., Fawcett Place, Greenwich, Conn. 06830.

Subsidiary Organization

Section 18. Should it be desired by any number of members to stimulate special activity and development in any particular branch of art and letters, a board or association may be formed for that purpose by presenting to the board of directors a petition signed by eight members, and if the petition is approved, a meeting is called by the secretary of all members whose interest in the project is likely to be enlisted. Should the formation of such an organization meet with favorable consideration of three-fifths of those who attend the meeting, the board of directors shall issue a certificate of organization which shall be signed by the president and secretary, and bear the organization's seal. Rules for the governing of its members, and which are in no sense in conflict with those of the organization as an entire body, may be adopted by any subsidiary organization.

Section 19. Upon a petition of three-fifths of the members of any subsidiary organization, such organization may be dissolved by the board of directors; or for any cause subversive of the governing rules of this organization.

Section 20. A full report shall be submitted annually to the board of directors of this organization by all subsidiary organizations.

Quorum

Section 21. At any regular meeting of this organization one-eighth of the members present shall constitute a quorum.

Amendments

Section 22. By a three-fifths vote at any meeting of this organization, these by-laws may be amended, if previously notice of the proposed amendment has been approved by the board of directors, posted on the bulletin board, and mailed to each member by the secretary, at least one week before the time to vote.

Standing Rules

1. Members shall be limited in speaking on a single question to not oftener than three times, and for no longer than ten minutes each time.
2. Except upon the invitation of the board of directors, none others than members shall address this organization.
3. Written resolutions only may be presented.

Concluding Remarks

A Few Suggestions to Presiding Officers

In bringing this book to a close, it will not be out of place to make a suggestion or two for the benefit of those persons who may be called upon to act as presiding officers for the first time.

Close Attention to Proceedings Essential

One of the most essential parts of the duty of a presiding officer is, to give the closest attention to the proceedings of the assembly, and, especially, to what is said by every member who speaks. Without the first, confusion will be almost certain to occur; wasting the time, perhaps disturbing the harmony, of the assembly. The latter is not merely a decent manifestation of respect for those who have elevated him to an honorable station, but it tends greatly to encourage timid or difficult members, and to secure them a patient and attentive hearing; and it often enables the presiding officer, by a timely interference, to check offensive language and to prevent scenes of tumult and disorder, such as have sometimes disgraced our legislative halls.

Strict Adherence to Rules Enjoined upon Presiding Officer

It should be constantly kept in mind by a presiding officer that in a deliberative assembly there can regularly be but one thing done or doing at the same time. This caution he will find particularly useful to him whenever a quarrel arises between two members in consequence of words spoken in debate. In such a case he will do well to require that the regular course of proceedings shall be strictly pursued, and will take care to restrain members from interfering in any other manner. In general, the solemnity and deliberation of the presiding officer will do much to allay heat and excitement, and to restore harmony and order in the assembly.

The Great Purpose of All Rules

A presiding officer will often find himself embarrassed by the difficulty, as well as the delicacy, of deciding points of order, or giving directions as to the manner of proceeding. In such cases it will be useful for him to recollect that—

The great purpose of all rules and forms is to subserve the will of the assembly, rather than to restrain it; to facilitate, and not to obstruct, the expression of their deliberate sense.